RENO

TRAVEL GUIDE

The Ultimate Guide to the Biggest Little City

Louis Bellisario

TABLE OF CONTENTS

THIS TRAVEL GUIDE IS PRESENTED WITHOUT IMAGES, BUT IT HAS BEEN METICULOUSLY CRAFTED TO ENHANCE YOUR TOURING EXPERIENCE.

Designed as a companion, it aims to provide an unforgettable journey by highlighting must-visit places and activities. Extensive research has been conducted to ensure the guidebook offers a top-notch experience for users.

While the guide endeavors to maintain accuracy, users are encouraged to utilize Google Maps for precise mapping and directions to their chosen destinations. Despite the dedicated effort to ensure accuracy, users are advised to exercise discretion when implementing the advice and recommendations found in this guide. Unforeseen changes to costs, opening hours, and other details may occur.

When making travel arrangements, plans, or bookings, it is advisable to consult relevant authorities, companies, online resources or organizations. This guide serves as a companion to enrich your experience upon arrival at your travel destination, and establishments, goods, and services mentioned herein are recommendations based on the author's personal and popular experiences, not endorsements.

Finally, users are urged to adhere to local laws and customs, exercise caution, and prioritize safety while enjoying their amazing travel experience.

INTRODUCTION

Welcome to Reno, the vibrant heart of Northern Nevada, where the spirit of the Wild West meets the excitement of modern entertainment. Nestled against the backdrop of the Sierra Nevada mountains and the Truckee River, Reno offers a captivating blend of natural beauty, cultural richness, and exhilarating experiences.

Discovering Reno:

Reno isn't just a destination; it's an experience waiting to unfold. As you wander through its bustling streets and iconic landmarks, you'll encounter a city pulsating with energy and possibility. From the glittering lights of the famous casinos to the tranquil beauty of its parks and outdoor spaces, Reno promises something for every traveler.

A Rich Tapestry of History:

Steeped in history and tradition, Reno boasts a fascinating past that echoes through its streets and buildings. Once a humble railroad town, it rose to prominence during the silver mining boom of the late 19th century. Today, remnants of its storied past can be found in its historic districts, museums, and preserved landmarks, offering a glimpse into its bygone era.

Unraveling Reno's Charms:

This travel guide is your key to unlocking the treasures of Reno. Whether you're drawn to the thrill of the gaming tables, eager to explore its cultural attractions, or simply craving a taste of its renowned culinary scene, we've got you covered. From the glittering lights of downtown to the laid-back vibe of its neighborhoods, we'll guide you through every corner of this dynamic city.

What to Expect:

In the following pages, you'll find comprehensive information on everything Reno has to offer. From practical tips on transportation and accommodation to in-depth guides on attractions, dining, and nightlife, we've curated the ultimate resource to ensure you make the most of your visit. Whether you're a first-time visitor or a seasoned traveler, let us be your trusted companion on this unforgettable journey.

Embark on an Adventure:

So, pack your bags and prepare for an adventure like no other. Whether you're seeking thrills, relaxation, or a little bit of both, Reno is ready to welcome you with open arms. Let the excitement begin as we set off together to explore the wonders of this extraordinary city. Get ready to create memories that will last a lifetime as you embark on a journey of discovery through the vibrant streets of Reno.

CHAPTER 1

GETTING ACQUAINTED WITH RENO

Historical Background

Nestled in the picturesque Truckee Meadows, Reno's history is as diverse and colorful as the landscape that surrounds it. From its humble beginnings as a small trading post to its transformation into the bustling metropolis it is today, Reno's journey through time is a testament to resilience, innovation, and the pioneering spirit of the American West.

Origins and Early Settlement:

The story of Reno begins in the early 1850s when a group of prospectors stumbled upon the fertile valley that would later become known as the Truckee Meadows. Drawn by the promise of abundant water and fertile soil, settlers began to trickle into the area, laying the foundation for what would soon become a thriving community.

The Railroad Era:

Reno's fortunes changed dramatically with the arrival of the Central Pacific Railroad in 1868. As the railroad expanded westward, Reno emerged as a vital hub, connecting the booming mining towns of the Comstock Lode with the rest of the country. The completion of the Transcontinental Railroad in 1869 further solidified Reno's position as a strategic transportation center, fueling its rapid growth and development.

The Rise of the Gaming Industry:

In the early 20th century, Reno experienced another period of growth with the legalization of gambling in Nevada. As casinos and resorts began to dot the landscape, Reno earned a reputation as the "Biggest Little City in the World," drawing visitors from far and wide with promises of excitement and adventure. Today, the city's vibrant gaming industry continues to be a driving force in its economy and culture.

Cultural Influences:

Throughout its history, Reno has been shaped by a diverse array of cultural influences, from the indigenous peoples who first inhabited the region to the waves of immigrants who flocked here in search of fortune and opportunity. The city's cultural heritage is reflected in its architecture, cuisine, and traditions, creating a rich tapestry of experiences for visitors to explore.

Architectural Landmarks and Museums:

As you wander through the streets of Reno, you'll encounter a wealth of architectural landmarks that bear witness to its storied past. From the elegant Victorian mansions of the Old Southwest to the Art Deco splendor of downtown, each building tells a story of a bygone era. Museums such as the Nevada Museum of Art and the National Automobile Museum offer a glimpse into Reno's past, showcasing artifacts and exhibits that celebrate its cultural heritage.

Preserving the Past:

As Reno continues to evolve and grow, efforts are underway to preserve and celebrate its rich history. Historic preservation initiatives, archaeological excavations, and community events serve to honor the legacy of those who came before us, ensuring that Reno's unique heritage will be cherished for generations to come.

From its roots as a humble trading post to its current status as a vibrant metropolis, Reno's journey through history is a testament to the resilience and spirit of its people. As you explore the city's streets and landmarks, take a moment to reflect on the countless generations who have called this place home and the enduring legacy they have left behind. In Reno, the past is not just a memory—it's a living, breathing part of the present, waiting to be discovered and celebrated by all who visit.

Cultural Diversity

Nestled within the rugged beauty of Northern Nevada, Reno is a melting pot of cultures, traditions, and influences. From its vibrant arts scene to its eclectic culinary landscape, the city's rich tapestry of diversity is woven into every aspect of life, creating a dynamic and inclusive community that celebrates its differences while embracing its shared humanity.

Historical Context:

Reno's cultural diversity has deep roots that stretch back centuries. Native American tribes, including the Washoe, Paiute, and Shoshone, have inhabited the region for thousands of years, leaving behind a legacy of traditions and customs that continue to shape the city's identity. With the arrival of European settlers in the 19th century, Reno became a crossroads of cultures, as immigrants from around the world flocked to the area in search of opportunity and adventure.

Ethnic Communities:

Today, Reno is home to a vibrant array of ethnic communities, each contributing its own unique flavor to the city's cultural landscape. From the bustling Asian markets of Chinatown to the lively Hispanic neighborhoods of East Fourth Street, the city is a patchwork of traditions, languages, and cuisines that reflect the diversity of its residents.

Arts and Entertainment:

Reno's cultural diversity is perhaps most visible in its thriving arts and entertainment scene. From galleries showcasing the works of local artists to theaters hosting performances from around the world, the city offers a wealth of opportunities to experience the richness of global culture. Annual events such as the Reno Artown Festival and the Great Italian Festival celebrate the city's multicultural heritage, bringing together people from all walks of life to revel in the joy of creativity and expression.

Cuisine:

Food is another vibrant expression of Reno's cultural diversity, with a culinary scene that spans the globe. From traditional Basque eateries serving up hearty comfort food to trendy fusion restaurants blending flavors from East and West, the city's dining options are as diverse as its population. Food festivals, such as the Eldorado Great Italian Festival and the Biggest Little City Wing Fest, offer a delicious glimpse into the culinary traditions of Reno's diverse communities.

Community Engagement:

Reno's cultural diversity isn't just a source of entertainment—it's a way of life. Community organizations, cultural centers, and grassroots initiatives work tirelessly to promote understanding, appreciation, and respect among the city's residents. Through festivals, workshops, and educational programs, they foster a sense of unity and belonging that transcends cultural boundaries, enriching the lives of all who call Reno home.

In Reno, cultural diversity isn't just celebrated—it's embraced as a fundamental part of what makes the city great. From its vibrant arts scene to its eclectic culinary landscape, the city's rich tapestry of cultures and traditions serves as a source of inspiration, creativity, and connection for residents and visitors alike. As you explore the streets of Reno, take a moment to savor the sights, sounds, and flavors of this diverse and dynamic community, and celebrate the beauty of our shared humanity.

Geography and Location

Nestled in the picturesque Sierra Nevada mountains of Northern Nevada, Reno is a vibrant city with a stunning natural backdrop. Its strategic location and diverse geography make it a unique destination for outdoor enthusiasts, history buffs, and urban adventurers alike.

Mountain Majesty:

Reno's proximity to the Sierra Nevada mountains shapes both its geography and its character. Towering peaks, including the iconic Mount Rose, loom on the horizon, offering a breathtaking backdrop for outdoor activities year-round. In winter, the nearby ski resorts of Lake Tahoe beckon with pristine slopes and world-class amenities, while summer brings opportunities for hiking, mountain biking, and rock climbing in the surrounding wilderness areas.

Desert Oasis:

Despite its mountainous surroundings, Reno lies in the heart of the Great Basin Desert, a vast expanse of arid terrain that stretches across much of the American West. The city's high desert climate is characterized by hot, dry summers and cold, snowy winters, creating a diverse ecosystem that supports a wide range of plant and animal life. From the sagebrush-studded foothills to the cottonwood-lined banks of the Truckee River, Reno's natural landscapes are as varied as they are beautiful.

Urban Hub:

Located just east of the California border, Reno serves as a gateway to the Sierra Nevada region, attracting visitors from near and far with its unique blend of outdoor adventure and urban sophistication. The city's downtown area is a bustling hub of activity, with a vibrant arts scene, diverse dining options, and a thriving nightlife that rivals that of much larger cities. Cultural attractions such as museums, theaters, and galleries offer opportunities for exploration and discovery, while historic landmarks and architectural gems provide glimpses into Reno's storied past.

Transportation Hub:

Reno's central location and excellent transportation infrastructure make it easily accessible from all directions. The city is served by Reno-Tahoe International Airport, offering direct flights to major cities across the United States. Interstate 80, one of the country's primary east-west thoroughfares, passes through the city, providing convenient access for travelers arriving by car or bus. Additionally, Amtrak operates daily train service to Reno from cities such as Sacramento and Salt Lake City, making it an accessible destination for visitors from throughout the region.

With its stunning natural beauty, diverse geography, and convenient location, Reno offers something for everyone. Whether you're seeking outdoor adventure in the mountains, exploring the city's vibrant cultural scene, or simply enjoying the breathtaking scenery, Reno is a destination that captivates the imagination and invites exploration. So pack your bags, hit the road, and get ready to discover all that Reno has to offer. Adventure awaits!

Climate Overview

Reno enjoys a high desert climate, characterized by its sunny days, low humidity, and dramatic temperature fluctuations between day and night. Situated in the Great Basin region of Nevada, the city experiences distinct seasonal changes, each offering its own unique opportunities for outdoor recreation and exploration.

Summer (June to August):

Summers in Reno are typically warm and dry, with plenty of sunshine and clear blue skies. Daytime temperatures often soar into the 90s°F (32-37°C), occasionally reaching above 100°F (38°C) during heatwaves. Despite the heat, the low humidity levels provide relief, making outdoor activities such as hiking, biking, and water sports enjoyable. Evenings bring cooler temperatures, dropping into the 50s and 60s°F (10-20°C), offering pleasant conditions for outdoor dining and entertainment.

Fall (September to November):

Fall in Reno brings milder temperatures and crisp, clear days. Daytime highs gradually decrease from the 80s°F (27-32°C) in September to the 60s°F (15-20°C) by November. Cool evenings signal the changing season, with temperatures dipping into the 30s and 40s°F (0-10°C). Fall foliage adds a splash of color to the surrounding landscapes, making it an ideal time for scenic drives, hiking, and exploring the region's natural beauty.

Winter (December to February):

Winter in Reno is characterized by cold temperatures and occasional snowfall. Daytime highs typically range from the 40s to the 50s°F (4-10°C), while nighttime lows can plummet below freezing, often dipping into the 20s°F (-6 to -1°C). Snow is common in the surrounding mountains, creating ideal conditions for skiing, snowboarding, and other winter sports at nearby resorts like Lake Tahoe. In the city, snowfall is less frequent but still possible, adding a festive touch to the holiday season.

Spring (March to May):

Springtime in Reno brings a burst of color as wildflowers bloom across the desert landscape. Temperatures gradually warm up, with daytime highs climbing from the 50s to the 70s°F (10-25°C) by May. Nights remain cool, with temperatures ranging from the 30s to the 50s°F (0-15°C). Spring is an excellent time to explore Reno's outdoor attractions, from hiking trails and botanical gardens to scenic drives and outdoor festivals celebrating the season's arrival.

Reno's high desert climate offers a diverse range of weather conditions throughout the year, providing ample opportunities for outdoor adventure and exploration. Whether you're skiing in the winter, hiking in the spring, enjoying water sports in the summer, or marveling at fall foliage, Reno's climate ensures that there's something for everyone to enjoy, no matter the season.

CHAPTER 2

PLANNING YOUR TRIP

Setting Your Reno Travel Goals

Planning a trip to Reno can be an exciting adventure filled with endless possibilities. Whether you're drawn to the glitz and glamour of the casinos, the outdoor adventures of the surrounding mountains, or the vibrant cultural scene of the city, defining your travel goals will help you make the most of your visit to the Biggest Little City in the World.

1. Define Your Interests:

Consider what aspects of Reno intrigue you the most. Are you interested in exploring the city's rich history and cultural heritage? Are you seeking outdoor thrills like skiing, hiking, or kayaking? Or perhaps you're looking forward to sampling the renowned cuisine and nightlife scene? Identifying your interests will guide your itinerary and ensure you focus on the experiences that matter most to you.

2. Set Priorities:

With so much to see and do in Reno, it's essential to prioritize your activities based on your interests and time constraints. Make a list of must-see attractions, activities, and experiences, then prioritize them according to your preferences. This will help you allocate your time and resources efficiently and ensure you don't miss out on anything that's important to you.

3. Establish Your Budget:

Determine how much you're willing to spend on your trip to Reno, including transportation, accommodation, dining, entertainment, and activities. Setting a budget will help you make informed decisions about where to splurge and where to save, ensuring you stay within your financial means while still enjoying all that Reno has to offer.

4. Research and Plan:

Take the time to research Reno's attractions, activities, and events to create a comprehensive itinerary that aligns with your travel goals. Explore the city's top landmarks, outdoor adventures, cultural attractions, dining hotspots, and entertainment venues, and map out your days accordingly. Consider factors such as operating hours, admission prices, and seasonal events to optimize your experience.

5. Be Flexible:

While it's essential to have a plan in place, be open to spontaneity and unexpected discoveries along the way. Leave room in your itinerary for impromptu adventures, hidden gems, and serendipitous experiences that may arise during your time in Reno. Embrace the freedom to explore and adapt your plans as you go, allowing yourself to truly immerse in the moment and make memories that will last a lifetime.

By setting clear travel goals and planning thoughtfully, you'll be well-prepared to embark on an unforgettable journey to Reno, where endless excitement and adventure await at every turn. Whether you're seeking relaxation, adventure, or a bit of both, Reno offers a wealth of experiences to satisfy every traveler's wanderlust.

Choosing the Best Time to Visit

Selecting the ideal time to visit Reno depends on your preferences, interests, and desired experiences. Each season offers unique opportunities and attractions, so consider the following factors when planning your trip:

1. Weather:

- Summer (June to August): Warm temperatures and sunny skies make summer an excellent time for outdoor activities like hiking, biking, and water sports. However, it can get quite hot during the day, so be prepared for high temperatures.
- Fall (September to November): Fall brings cooler temperatures and vibrant foliage to the region, making it ideal for scenic drives, outdoor adventures, and exploring the city's cultural attractions.
- Winter (December to February): Winter in Reno means snowy landscapes and opportunities for skiing, snowboarding, and other winter sports in the nearby mountains. The city also hosts festive events and holiday celebrations during this time.
- Spring (March to May): Springtime brings mild temperatures and blooming wildflowers to the area, making it perfect for outdoor activities like hiking, biking, and exploring the city's parks and gardens.

2. Events and Festivals:

- Check Reno's event calendar for festivals, concerts, and special events happening throughout the year. From the Reno Rodeo in June to the Great Reno Balloon Race in

September, there's always something exciting happening in the city.

- Consider timing your visit to coincide with events that align with your interests, whether it's music, food, art, or outdoor adventure.

3. Crowds and Prices:

- Peak tourist seasons in Reno typically coincide with major events, holidays, and school breaks. Expect larger crowds and higher prices for accommodations and activities during these times.
- If you prefer a quieter experience and lower prices, consider visiting during the shoulder seasons (spring and fall) when tourist traffic is lighter, but the weather is still pleasant.

4. Outdoor Activities:

- The best time for outdoor activities in Reno depends on your interests. Skiing and snowboarding are popular in the winter months, while hiking, biking, and water sports are ideal during the warmer months.
- Consider the weather conditions and seasonal closures when planning outdoor adventures, and be prepared with appropriate gear and clothing.

5. Personal Preferences:

- Ultimately, the best time to visit Reno is when it aligns with your interests, preferences, and schedule. Whether you're seeking winter sports, summer adventures, or cultural experiences, Reno offers something for every traveler year-round.

By considering these factors and weighing your options, you can choose the best time to visit Reno and ensure an unforgettable experience filled with adventure, exploration, and excitement.

Visa and Entry Requirements

For travelers planning a visit to Reno, Nevada, it's essential to understand the visa and entry requirements for entry into the United States. Here's what you need to know:

1. Visa Waiver Program (VWP):

- Citizens of participating countries may be eligible to travel to the United States for tourism or business purposes without obtaining a visa under the Visa Waiver Program.
- Travelers must apply for authorization through the Electronic System for Travel Authorization (ESTA) before entering the United States.
- ESTA approval must be obtained at least 72 hours before travel and is valid for multiple entries into the United States for up to two years.

2. Visitor Visa (B-2):

- Travelers from countries not eligible for the Visa Waiver Program or those planning to stay longer than 90 days must apply for a B-2 visitor visa.
- The B-2 visa is for tourism, pleasure, or visiting friends and relatives in the United States.
- Applicants must schedule an interview at a U.S. embassy or consulate in their home country, complete the visa application form (DS-160), and provide supporting documents, such as a valid passport, travel itinerary, and proof of funds.

3. Passport Requirements:

- All travelers entering the United States, regardless of visa status, must possess a valid passport that expires at least six months beyond their intended period of stay.
- It's essential to ensure your passport is in good condition and has enough blank pages for entry stamps.

4. Customs and Border Protection (CBP) Requirements:

- Upon arrival in the United States, travelers must undergo inspection by U.S. Customs and Border Protection (CBP) officers at their port of entry.
- Be prepared to present your passport, visa (if applicable), ESTA approval (if applicable), and any supporting documents requested by CBP officers.
- Answer questions about the purpose of your visit, your intended length of stay, and any items you are bringing into the country.

5. Traveler's Responsibilities:

- It's the responsibility of each traveler to ensure they meet the entry requirements for the United States and possess the necessary documentation for their trip.
- Familiarize yourself with U.S. entry regulations, including restrictions on prohibited items and substances.
- Be truthful and cooperative during CBP inspections, as providing false information or attempting to enter the country illegally can result in serious consequences, including denial of entry and deportation.

6. Additional Requirements:

- Travelers may be subject to additional entry requirements or restrictions due to public health concerns, security concerns, or changes in immigration policy. It's essential to stay informed of any updates or changes that may affect your travel plans.

Before planning your trip to Reno, be sure to check the latest visa and entry requirements for the United States and consult with the nearest U.S. embassy or consulate for personalized guidance based on your individual circumstances. With proper planning and preparation, you can ensure a smooth and hassle-free entry into the United States and enjoy your visit to the vibrant city of Reno, Nevada.

Budgeting and Money Matters

Managing your finances effectively is key to enjoying a stress-free and budget-friendly trip to Reno. From currency exchange options to creating a travel budget and saving money on expenses, here's everything you need to know to make the most of your funds while exploring the Biggest Little City in the World.

Currency Exchange:

- Reno primarily uses the United States Dollar (USD). Currency exchange services are available at banks, currency exchange offices, and some hotels.
- Consider using ATMs to withdraw cash in USD, as they often offer competitive exchange rates. Be aware of any fees charged by your bank for international withdrawals.
- Credit cards are widely accepted in Reno, but it's advisable to inform your bank of your travel plans beforehand to avoid any issues with card usage.

Creating a Travel Budget:

- Estimate your expenses for accommodation, meals, transportation, activities, and souvenirs before your trip. Research average costs in Reno to help you plan your budget effectively.
- Allocate funds for emergencies or unexpected costs, such as medical expenses or transportation delays. It's recommended to set aside a portion of your budget as a contingency fund.
- Use budgeting tools and apps to track your expenses and stay within your budget during your trip. Adjust your spending as needed to avoid overspending.

Saving Money While Traveling:

- Utilize public transportation options, such as buses or rideshare services, to save on transportation costs. Consider purchasing multi-day passes for additional savings.
- Dine at local eateries and cafes to experience authentic cuisine at lower prices compared to tourist areas. Look for happy hour specials or prix fixe menus for budget-friendly dining options.
- Seek out free or discounted attractions, such as parks, museums with free admission days, or outdoor events and festivals. Take advantage of complimentary activities offered by your accommodation, such as fitness facilities or guided tours.
- Avoid unnecessary expenses by prioritizing experiences that align with your interests and skipping costly activities or attractions that don't add value to your trip.

Managing Finances Securely:

- Keep valuables, cash, and important documents secure at all times. Use a money belt or secure pouch to carry cash and passports, and consider using a hotel safe for additional security.
- Monitor your bank accounts and credit card transactions regularly to detect any unauthorized charges or fraudulent activity. Report any suspicious activity to your bank or credit card issuer immediately.
- Carry backup payment methods, such as a second credit card or traveler's checks, in case your primary payment method is lost, stolen, or declined.

By following these practical tips and strategies for managing your finances while traveling in Reno, you can make informed decisions, maximize your budget, and enjoy a memorable and budget-friendly trip to this vibrant city in the heart of Nevada.

Essential Packing Checklists

Packing for your trip to Reno requires careful consideration of the city's climate, activities, and your personal preferences. To ensure you have everything you need for a comfortable and enjoyable stay, here are essential packing checklists for both general items and specific activities:

General Packing Checklist:

Clothing:

- Casual attire for exploring the city, including comfortable walking shoes, jeans, and T-shirts.
- Lightweight layers for variable weather conditions, such as a sweater or jacket for cooler evenings.

- Swimwear and sandals if you plan to visit pools or hot springs.
- Dressier outfits for dining out or attending events.
- Undergarments, socks, and sleepwear.

Toiletries:

- Personal hygiene items, including toothbrush, toothpaste, shampoo, conditioner, soap, and deodorant.
- Skincare products, sunscreen, and lip balm with SPF for sun protection.
- Medications and first-aid supplies, including pain relievers, motion sickness medication, and any prescription medications you require.
- Hairbrush or comb, hair ties, and other styling tools.

Travel Essentials:

- Valid passport or government-issued ID.
- Travel documents, such as airline tickets, hotel reservations, and rental car information.
- Travel insurance information and emergency contact numbers.
- Cash, credit cards, and ATM/debit cards.
- Travel adapter and voltage converter for electronic devices.

Electronics:

- Smartphone and charger.
- Camera or smartphone for capturing memories.
- Portable charger or power bank for on-the-go charging.
- Headphones or earbuds for entertainment during travel.

Miscellaneous Items:

- Travel-sized umbrella or poncho for unexpected rain showers.
- Reusable water bottle to stay hydrated throughout the day.
- Snacks, such as granola bars or trail mix, for energy on the go.
- Daypack or tote bag for carrying essentials during sightseeing excursions.
- Guidebook or maps of Reno for navigating the city.

Activity-Specific Packing Checklist:

Outdoor Adventures:

- Hiking boots or sturdy walking shoes for trails in the Sierra Nevada mountains.
- Lightweight, moisture-wicking clothing for outdoor activities.
- Sun hat, sunglasses, and sunscreen for sun protection.
- Backpack with water bladder or water bottles for hydration on the trail.
- Trail snacks and a packed lunch for longer hikes.

Winter Sports:

- Ski or snowboard equipment, including skis, boots, poles, or snowboard, boots, and bindings.
- Warm, waterproof clothing, including insulated jacket, pants, gloves, and hat.
- Goggles or sunglasses with UV protection for snow glare.
- Hand and foot warmers for extra warmth in cold weather.

Casino and Nightlife:

- Dressy attire for evenings out, such as cocktail dresses or dress shirts and slacks.
- Comfortable shoes for dancing or walking between casinos.
- Small clutch or crossbody bag for carrying essentials.

Relaxation and Wellness:

- Yoga mat for practicing yoga or meditation.
- Bathing suit and towel for visiting hot springs or spas.
- Essential oils or aromatherapy products for relaxation.

By packing these essential items and tailoring your packing list to your planned activities and preferences, you'll be well-prepared for an unforgettable trip to Reno, Nevada.

Travel Friendly Luggage Options

Selecting the right luggage is essential for a smooth and enjoyable travel experience to Reno. With a wide range of options available, it's important to choose luggage that suits your needs, preferences, and travel style. Here's a guide to help you navigate the world of travel-friendly luggage options:

Types of Luggage:

Suitcases:

- Suitcases come in various sizes, from carry-on to large checked bags, and are typically designed with wheels and a telescopic handle for easy maneuverability.
- Hardshell suitcases provide durability and protection for your belongings, while softshell suitcases offer flexibility and expandability.

- Consider spinner suitcases with four multidirectional wheels for effortless navigation through airports and city streets.

Backpacks:

- Backpacks are ideal for travelers who prefer hands-free carrying and versatility.
- Look for backpacks with padded straps and back panels for comfort during extended wear, as well as multiple compartments and organizational features for easy access to your belongings.

Duffel Bags:

- Duffel bags are lightweight and flexible, making them perfect for short trips or as an additional bag for souvenirs.
- Choose duffel bags with sturdy handles and shoulder straps for comfortable carrying, and look for options with wheels for added convenience.

Carry-On Bags:

- Carry-on bags are designed to fit within airline size restrictions for overhead compartments or under-seat storage.
- Opt for carry-on bags with expandable compartments and organizational pockets to maximize space and keep your essentials easily accessible during your flight.

Factors to Consider:

Size and Weight:

- Choose luggage that meets the size and weight restrictions of your airline to avoid additional fees or inconvenience.
- Consider the length of your trip and the amount of belongings you need to pack when selecting luggage size.

Durability:

- Look for luggage made from durable materials, such as polycarbonate or ballistic nylon, to withstand the rigors of travel.
- Check the quality of zippers, handles, and wheels to ensure they can withstand frequent use.

Security Features:

- Prioritize luggage with built-in security features, such as TSA-approved locks or combination locks, to protect your belongings during transit.
- Consider using luggage straps or cable ties for added security and peace of mind.

Ease of Handling:

- Test the maneuverability of wheels and handles to ensure smooth navigation through airports and other travel hubs.
- Look for luggage with ergonomic handles and lightweight construction for ease of handling during transit.

Packing Techniques and Organization Tips:

Use Packing Cubes:

- Packing cubes help keep your belongings organized and compact, allowing you to maximize space and minimize wrinkles.

- Use different-colored packing cubes to differentiate between clothing items and accessories for easy retrieval.

Utilize Compression Bags:

- Compression bags are great for compressing bulky items like sweaters or jackets, allowing you to save space in your luggage.
- Roll your clothes instead of folding them to save space and prevent wrinkles.

Pack Efficiently:

- Pack heavier items at the bottom of your suitcase or backpack to distribute weight evenly and prevent tipping.
- Place shoes in plastic bags to protect clothing from dirt and odors, and utilize empty spaces within shoes for smaller items like socks or belts.

Travel Accessories and Gadgets:

Luggage Locks:

- Invest in TSA-approved luggage locks to secure your belongings while complying with airport security regulations.
- Consider using cable locks or retractable cable locks to secure your luggage to stationary objects for added security during transit.

Luggage Trackers:

- Luggage trackers allow you to monitor the location of your luggage in real-time using GPS technology, providing peace of mind in case of lost or delayed baggage.

- Choose luggage trackers with long battery life and user-friendly mobile apps for easy tracking and management.

By considering these factors and incorporating packing techniques and organization tips into your travel preparations, you can select the best luggage options for your trip to Reno and ensure a stress-free and enjoyable travel experience. Whether you prefer the convenience of a suitcase, the versatility of a backpack, or the flexibility of a duffel bag, there's a travel-friendly luggage option to suit every traveler's needs and preferences.

Itinerary Suggestion: Duration of Stay

Reno, known as the "Biggest Little City in the World," offers a plethora of attractions and activities to suit every traveler's interests and preferences. Whether you're a nature enthusiast, a history buff, a thrill-seeker, or a foodie, Reno has something to offer for everyone. Here are itinerary suggestions for different types of travelers, including recommended durations of stay and detailed activities to explore:

1. Nature Enthusiasts:

Duration of Stay: 3-5 Days

Day 1:

- Start your journey with a visit to Lake Tahoe, just a short drive from Reno. Explore the pristine waters of the lake, go kayaking, paddleboarding, or simply relax on the beach.
- Take a scenic drive along the Lake Tahoe Loop, stopping at overlooks and viewpoints to admire the breathtaking vistas of the surrounding mountains.

- In the evening, return to Reno and enjoy a leisurely stroll along the Truckee River Walk, a scenic pathway that meanders along the banks of the Truckee River.

Day 2:

- Embark on a hiking adventure in the Sierra Nevada mountains. Choose from a variety of trails ranging from easy walks to challenging treks, such as the Hunter Creek Trail or the Mount Rose Summit Trail.
- Visit the Animal Ark Wildlife Sanctuary to observe native wildlife species up close, including wolves, bears, and birds of prey.
- End your day with a visit to the Reno Riverwalk District, where you can dine at waterfront restaurants or browse boutique shops and galleries.

Day 3:

- Spend a day exploring the Great Basin National Park, located a few hours' drive from Reno. Discover ancient bristlecone pine forests, explore limestone caves, and hike to the summit of Wheeler Peak for panoramic views of the surrounding desert landscape.
- On your way back to Reno, stop at the historic town of Virginia City to experience the Old West charm and learn about the area's rich mining history.

2. History Buffs:

Duration of Stay: 2-4 Days

Day 1:

- Begin your exploration of Reno's history with a visit to the Nevada Museum of Art, where you can admire a diverse collection of artworks inspired by the American West.
- Take a guided tour of the Nevada State Capitol Building in nearby Carson City to learn about the state's political history and architecture.
- In the evening, attend a performance at the historic Pioneer Center for the Performing Arts, which hosts concerts, theater productions, and dance performances throughout the year.

Day 2:

- Explore Reno's vibrant cultural scene with a visit to the National Automobile Museum, home to a vast collection of vintage cars and automotive memorabilia.
- Step back in time with a visit to the Nevada Historical Society Museum, where you can learn about the state's pioneer history, Native American heritage, and mining boom era.
- Take a self-guided walking tour of the Historic Fourth Ward School Museum in Virginia City, a preserved 19th-century schoolhouse that offers insights into the town's past.

Day 3 (Optional):

- Extend your stay to include a day trip to the Comstock Gold Mill in Virginia City, where you can tour a historic stamp mill and learn about the process of extracting gold from ore.
- Visit the Reno Arch, an iconic landmark that has welcomed visitors to the city since the 1920s, and take a stroll through

downtown Reno to admire its collection of historic buildings and public art installations.

3. Thrill-Seekers:

Duration of Stay: 2-3 Days

Day 1:

- Kick off your adrenaline-fueled adventure with a visit to the Grand Sierra Resort's Grand Adventure Land, where you can ride thrilling attractions such as the zipline, go-karts, and bungee jumping.
- Test your luck at one of Reno's many casinos, where you can try your hand at table games, slot machines, and poker tournaments.
- Enjoy a night of entertainment at one of Reno's top nightlife venues, such as the LEX Nightclub or the EDGE Nightclub at the Peppermill Resort.

Day 2:

- Experience the ultimate thrill with a skydiving adventure over the scenic landscapes of Reno and Lake Tahoe. Tandem skydiving options are available for beginners, allowing you to experience the rush of freefall under the guidance of an experienced instructor.
- Take a whitewater rafting trip down the Truckee River, navigating through Class II and III rapids while enjoying stunning views of the surrounding mountains.
- Unwind after your adventures with a relaxing soak in one of Reno's natural hot springs, such as the Steamboat Hot Springs or the David Walley's Hot Springs Resort.

4. Foodies:

Duration of Stay: 2-4 Days

Day 1:

- Begin your culinary journey with a food tour of downtown Reno, where you can sample a variety of local specialties, including Basque cuisine, craft beers, and artisanal chocolates.
- Visit the Reno Riverwalk District to dine at waterfront restaurants offering farm-to-table dishes, fresh seafood, and international cuisine with a local twist.
- End your day with a visit to the Reno Food Truck Friday event, held weekly during the summer months, where you can indulge in gourmet street food from a variety of vendors.

Day 2:

- Explore Reno's burgeoning craft beer scene with a brewery tour, where you can sample locally brewed beers and learn about the brewing process from expert brewers.
- Visit the Reno Midtown District, a hip and eclectic neighborhood known for its diverse dining options, including trendy cafes, gastropubs, and ethnic eateries.
- Attend a cooking class or culinary workshop to learn new skills and techniques from local chefs, such as pasta-making, wine pairing, or chocolate truffle making.

Day 3 (Optional):

- Extend your stay to include a day trip to the nearby town of Fallon, known as the "Oasis of Nevada," where you can visit local farms, orchards, and wineries to sample fresh produce, wines, and artisanal products.

- Explore Reno's farmers' markets, such as the Reno Farmers Market or the Midtown Farmers Market, to shop for locally grown fruits, vegetables, and gourmet treats to take home as souvenirs.

No matter what type of traveler you are, Reno offers an abundance of experiences and attractions to suit your interests and preferences. Whether you're seeking outdoor adventures, cultural discoveries, thrilling entertainment, or culinary delights, Reno promises an unforgettable journey filled with excitement and exploration.

CHAPTER 3

TRANSPORTATION OPTIONS

Getting to Reno

By Air

Reno, Nevada, is conveniently accessible by air, with several major airports serving the region and offering a wide range of flight options from various destinations. Here's a detailed look at getting to Reno, including major airports, airlines operating in and out of Reno, popular routes, average flight duration, and unique offerings:

1. Major Airports Serving Reno:

Reno-Tahoe International Airport (RNO): Located just a few miles southeast of downtown Reno, Reno-Tahoe International Airport is the primary airport serving the Reno-Sparks metropolitan area. The airport offers a modern terminal with a range of amenities and services for travelers, including dining options, retail shops, car rental agencies, and ground transportation options.

2. Airlines Operating in and out of Reno:

Reno-Tahoe International Airport is served by several major airlines, including:

- Southwest Airlines
- Alaska Airlines
- American Airlines
- Delta Air Lines
- United Airlines

Additionally, several regional carriers and charter airlines operate flights to and from Reno, providing a variety of options for travelers.

3. Popular Routes to Reno:

Reno-Tahoe International Airport offers nonstop flights to and from major cities across the United States, making it easy for travelers to reach Reno from various destinations. Some popular routes to Reno include:

- Los Angeles (LAX) to Reno (RNO)
- San Francisco (SFO) to Reno (RNO)
- Denver (DEN) to Reno (RNO)
- Phoenix (PHX) to Reno (RNO)
- Seattle (SEA) to Reno (RNO)

These routes are served by multiple airlines, providing flexibility and choice for travelers.

4. Average Flight Duration:

The flight duration to Reno varies depending on the departure city and routing. On average, nonstop flights from major West Coast cities such as Los Angeles or San Francisco to Reno take approximately 1 to 2 hours. Flights from other regions may have longer durations, typically ranging from 2 to 4 hours with one or more layovers.

5. Unique Offerings at Reno-Tahoe International Airport:

Reno-Tahoe International Airport offers travelers a range of unique amenities and services to enhance their airport experience, including:

- The Reno-Tahoe Marketplace: A retail area featuring local shops and boutiques offering a variety of goods, including locally made crafts, souvenirs, and gifts.
- Art Installations: The airport showcases rotating art installations and exhibits featuring works by local and regional artists, providing travelers with a glimpse of Reno's vibrant arts scene.
- Outdoor Observation Deck: Enjoy views of the Sierra Nevada mountains and aircraft take-offs and landings from the airport's outdoor observation deck, a unique feature that allows travelers to soak in the scenery before or after their flights.
- Gaming Lounge: For those looking to get into the Reno spirit right away, the airport offers a gaming lounge where travelers can try their luck at slot machines and other casino games before departing.

With its convenient airport facilities, diverse range of airlines and routes, and unique offerings, getting to Reno is a seamless and enjoyable experience for travelers from near and far. Whether you're arriving for outdoor adventures, gaming excitement, or cultural exploration, Reno-Tahoe International Airport welcomes you to the Biggest Little City in the World with open arms and a warm Western hospitality.

By Road

Traveling to Reno by road offers a scenic and flexible option for visitors coming from nearby cities or exploring the beautiful landscapes of the American West. Whether you're embarking on a road trip or driving from a neighboring state, here's a detailed guide on how to reach Reno by road, including major highways, driving routes, approximate driving times, and points of interest along the way:

1. Major Highways Leading to Reno:

- Interstate 80 (I-80): Interstate 80 is the main east-west highway that connects Reno with major cities on the West Coast, including San Francisco, Sacramento, and Salt Lake City. It traverses through the Sierra Nevada mountains and offers scenic views of the surrounding landscapes.
- US Route 395 (US-395): US-395 is a north-south highway that passes through Eastern California and Eastern Oregon before entering Nevada. It provides access to Reno from cities such as Carson City, Bishop, and Mammoth Lakes, offering opportunities to explore charming towns and natural attractions along the way.

2. Driving Routes to Reno:

- From San Francisco, California (via I-80): Take I-80 East from San Francisco, passing through Sacramento and traversing the Sierra Nevada mountains before reaching Reno. The approximate driving time from San Francisco to Reno is about 3.5 to 4 hours, depending on traffic and road conditions.
- From Los Angeles, California (via I-15 and I-395): Take I-15 North from Los Angeles, then merge onto I-395 North near Hesperia. Follow I-395 through the Eastern Sierra region, passing through towns like Bishop and Bridgeport, before reaching Reno. The approximate driving time from Los Angeles to Reno is about 7 to 8 hours, depending on traffic and stops along the way.

- From Salt Lake City, Utah (via I-80): Take I-80 West from Salt Lake City, passing through scenic landscapes of Utah and Nevada before reaching Reno. The approximate driving time from Salt Lake City to Reno is about 8 to 9 hours, depending on traffic and road conditions.

3. Points of Interest Along the Way:

- Lake Tahoe: Consider taking a detour to visit Lake Tahoe, a stunning alpine lake located about 30 miles south of Reno. Enjoy outdoor activities such as hiking, boating, or simply relaxing on the shores of the lake.
- Virginia City: Make a stop in Virginia City, a historic mining town located about 20 miles southeast of Reno. Explore its charming streets lined with 19th-century buildings, visit museums, and take a ride on the historic Virginia & Truckee Railroad.
- Truckee River Scenic Byway: Drive along the Truckee River Scenic Byway, which follows the Truckee River from Lake Tahoe to Reno. Enjoy scenic vistas, picnic spots, and opportunities for fishing and whitewater rafting along the way.

4. Travel Tips for Road Trippers:

- Plan your route in advance and check for any road closures, construction, or traffic updates along the way.
- Take breaks to rest and stretch your legs, especially during long drives. Consider stopping at scenic viewpoints or rest areas to enjoy the surroundings.
- Pack essentials for your road trip, including snacks, water, a first-aid kit, and emergency supplies.

- Observe traffic laws and drive safely, especially in mountainous areas where road conditions may vary.

Embark on a memorable road trip to Reno and enjoy the journey through stunning landscapes, charming towns, and endless adventures along the way. Whether you're seeking outdoor recreation, historic exploration, or simply a scenic drive, traveling to Reno by road promises an unforgettable experience filled with excitement and discovery.

By Rail

Traveling to Reno by train offers a nostalgic and leisurely alternative to conventional modes of transportation. While direct train service to Reno is limited, there are several scenic routes that allow travelers to arrive at nearby cities before completing their journey to Reno. Here's a comprehensive guide on how to reach Reno by train, including major train routes, connecting cities, approximate travel times, and the unique experience of train travel:

1. Amtrak Routes Serving Reno:

- California Zephyr (Chicago to Emeryville/San Francisco): The California Zephyr is one of Amtrak's most scenic routes, traversing through the heart of the Rocky Mountains and the Sierra Nevada mountains before reaching the San Francisco Bay Area. Travelers can disembark at the Emeryville station and transfer to a connecting bus or shuttle service to complete the journey to Reno.
- Coast Starlight (Seattle/Los Angeles to Emeryville): The Coast Starlight offers breathtaking views of the Pacific Coastline and Cascade Range as it travels between Seattle and Los Angeles. Travelers can disembark at the

Emeryville station and transfer to a connecting bus or shuttle service to reach Reno.

2. Connecting Cities and Travel Times:

From Emeryville, California: Travelers can take a connecting bus or shuttle service from Emeryville to Reno, with an approximate travel time of 4 to 5 hours depending on traffic and road conditions. Emeryville is located about 200 miles southwest of Reno.

3. Unique Experience of Train Travel:

- Scenic Views: Train travel offers passengers the opportunity to enjoy panoramic views of landscapes that are inaccessible by other modes of transportation. From snow-capped mountains to rolling hills and vast plains, the journey to Reno by train promises stunning vistas at every turn.
- Comfort and Relaxation: Sit back, relax, and enjoy the comforts of train travel, including spacious seating, ample legroom, and the freedom to move around and stretch your legs. Traveling by train allows passengers to unwind and enjoy the journey at a leisurely pace.
- Social Interaction: Train travel fosters social interaction and camaraderie among passengers, providing opportunities to meet fellow travelers, exchange stories, and share experiences along the way. Whether you're enjoying a meal in the dining car or striking up a conversation in the observation lounge, train travel brings people together in a unique and memorable way.

4. Tips for Train Travelers:

- Book in Advance: Reserve your train tickets and any connecting services in advance to secure the best fares and ensure availability, especially during peak travel seasons.
- Pack Essentials: Bring along essentials for your journey, including snacks, water, entertainment, and any personal items you may need during the trip.
- Arrive Early: Arrive at the train station early to allow time for check-in, boarding, and familiarizing yourself with the station facilities and amenities.
- Enjoy the Journey: Embrace the slower pace of train travel and take the time to appreciate the scenery, engage with fellow passengers, and savor the experience of traveling by rail.

Embark on a memorable journey to Reno by train and relive the golden era of rail travel as you traverse through breathtaking landscapes and charming towns along the way. Whether you're seeking adventure, relaxation, or simply a scenic escape, traveling to Reno by train promises an unforgettable experience filled with nostalgia and discovery.

Getting Around in Reno

Public Transportation

Getting around Reno is convenient and hassle-free with a variety of public transportation options available to residents and visitors alike. Whether you're exploring downtown attractions, venturing into surrounding neighborhoods, or commuting to nearby towns, here's a detailed guide to public transportation in Reno, including routes, schedules, and fare information:

1. RTC RIDE (Regional Transportation Commission):

- Bus Service: RTC RIDE operates a comprehensive bus network that serves Reno, Sparks, and surrounding areas. The bus system consists of multiple routes covering major thoroughfares, neighborhoods, and commercial districts throughout the region.
- Routes and Schedules: RTC RIDE offers a variety of routes with frequent service throughout the day, including weekdays, weekends, and holidays. Schedules vary by route and time of day, so be sure to check the RTC website or mobile app for the latest information on routes, schedules, and real-time arrivals.
- Fare Information: RTC RIDE fares are affordable and based on a flat rate for single rides. Discounted fares are available for seniors, students, and individuals with disabilities. Passes and fare cards can be purchased onboard buses or at designated sales outlets throughout the city.

2. RTC RAPID (Regional Transportation Commission):

- Bus Rapid Transit (BRT): RTC RAPID is a bus rapid transit system that provides fast, frequent, and reliable service along key corridors in Reno and Sparks. BRT vehicles feature enhanced amenities such as dedicated bus lanes, level boarding platforms, and real-time information displays.
- Routes and Schedules: RTC RAPID operates on designated routes with limited stops, offering efficient service for commuters and travelers. Schedules are available online or through the RTC mobile app, with frequent departures during peak hours and reduced service during off-peak times.

- Fare Information: RTC RAPID fares are consistent with RTC RIDE fares and can be paid using the same fare cards and passes. Cash fares are also accepted onboard buses, although exact change is required.

3. RTC ACCESS (Regional Transportation Commission):

- Paratransit Service: RTC ACCESS is a specialized door-to-door transportation service for individuals with disabilities who are unable to use traditional fixed-route buses. ACCESS vehicles are equipped with wheelchair lifts or ramps and provide personalized assistance for passengers.
- Service Area: RTC ACCESS operates within designated service areas in Reno and Sparks, covering a radius around fixed-route bus stops and major destinations. Reservations are required for ACCESS service, and trips must be scheduled in advance.
- Fare Information: RTC ACCESS fares are consistent with RTC RIDE fares and are based on a flat rate for eligible passengers. Personal care attendants accompanying riders may travel free of charge. Fare cards and passes can be used for RTC ACCESS trips.

Navigating Reno's public transportation system is easy and affordable, allowing travelers to explore the city and beyond with convenience and peace of mind. Whether you're commuting to work, running errands, or sightseeing around town, RTC RIDE, RTC RAPID, and RTC ACCESS provide reliable and accessible transportation options for all.

Taxis and Ridesharing

Reno offers a range of convenient and flexible transportation options through taxis and ridesharing services. These services provide an efficient way to get around the city, whether you're heading to a casino, exploring local attractions, or traveling to and from the airport. Here's a detailed guide on the availability, use, and approximate costs of taxis and ridesharing services in Reno, along with unique considerations and regulations.

1. Taxis in Reno:

Availability:

- Taxis are readily available throughout Reno, particularly in high-traffic areas such as downtown, the Reno-Tahoe International Airport, major hotels, and casinos. You can hail a taxi on the street, find them at designated taxi stands, or book one in advance through a phone call or mobile app.

Popular Taxi Companies:

Some of the well-known taxi companies operating in Reno include:

- Reno-Sparks Cab Company
- Yellow Cab of Reno
- Whittlesea Checker Taxi

Approximate Costs:

Taxi fares in Reno are regulated, and the cost typically includes a base fare plus a per-mile charge. Here are some approximate costs:

- Base fare: $3.50
- Per mile: $2.50
- Waiting time: $30 per hour

For example, a 5-mile trip from downtown Reno to the Reno-Tahoe International Airport would cost around $16-$18, excluding any additional waiting time or tips.

Payment Options:

- Taxis in Reno generally accept both cash and credit/debit cards. It's always a good idea to confirm the payment methods with the driver before starting your journey.

2. Ridesharing Services in Reno:

Availability:

Ridesharing services like Uber and Lyft operate extensively in Reno. These services can be easily accessed through their respective mobile apps, which allow you to request a ride, track the driver's arrival, and pay through the app.

How to Use Ridesharing Services:

- Download the Uber or Lyft app on your smartphone.
- Create an account and enter your payment information.
- Open the app, enter your destination, and request a ride.
- The app will show you the estimated fare and the driver's details.
- Confirm your ride and wait for your driver to arrive at the specified pickup location.

Approximate Costs:

Ridesharing costs in Reno vary based on factors such as distance, time of day, and demand. Here are some average costs:

- Base fare: $1.00 - $2.00
- Per mile: $1.00 - $1.50

- Per minute: $0.15 - $0.30

For example, a 5-mile trip from downtown Reno to the Reno-Tahoe International Airport would cost approximately $12-$15, depending on traffic and demand.

3. Unique Considerations and Regulations:

- Airport Pickup and Drop-off: Both taxis and ridesharing services are permitted to pick up and drop off passengers at the Reno-Tahoe International Airport. There are designated pickup zones for ridesharing services, so be sure to follow the signs and instructions in the app for the exact location.
- Safety and Security: Reno's taxis and ridesharing services are subject to regulations that ensure the safety and security of passengers. Licensed taxi drivers undergo background checks, and their vehicles are inspected regularly. Similarly, ridesharing services conduct background checks on their drivers and provide in-app safety features such as driver ratings, GPS tracking, and emergency assistance.
- Peak Times and Surge Pricing: During peak times, special events, or high demand periods, ridesharing services may implement surge pricing, which increases the fare. Always check the fare estimate in the app before confirming your ride to avoid unexpected costs.
- Tipping: Tipping is customary for both taxi drivers and rideshare drivers in Reno. While tipping is not mandatory, it's appreciated for good service. A standard tip is 10-15% of the fare, or you can round up to the nearest dollar.

Navigating Reno with taxis and ridesharing services offers flexibility and convenience, allowing you to explore the city at your own pace. Whether you're heading to a night out at a casino, exploring the beautiful outdoors, or simply getting around town, these transportation options provide reliable and efficient service to meet your needs.

Rental Cars

Renting a car in Reno provides the freedom and flexibility to explore the city and its surrounding attractions at your own pace. Whether you're planning a scenic road trip, visiting nearby Lake Tahoe, or simply need a convenient way to get around, here's a detailed guide on renting a car in Reno, including rental agencies, driving regulations, important considerations, popular road trip routes, and tips for navigating local traffic and parking.

Rental Car Agencies and Locations:

1. Major Rental Car Agencies:

Enterprise Rent-A-Car

- Locations: Reno-Tahoe International Airport, downtown Reno, and various neighborhood locations.

Hertz

- Locations: Reno-Tahoe International Airport and downtown Reno.

Avis

- Locations: Reno-Tahoe International Airport and several downtown locations.

Budget

- Locations: Reno-Tahoe International Airport and downtown Reno.

Alamo

- Locations: Reno-Tahoe International Airport.

National Car Rental

- Locations: Reno-Tahoe International Airport.

2. Airport Rental Car Center:

The Reno-Tahoe International Airport hosts several rental car agencies within its Rental Car Center, making it convenient for travelers to pick up and drop off their rental vehicles upon arrival or departure.

Driving Regulations:

1. Speed Limits:

- Urban Areas: Generally 25-35 mph.
- Residential Areas: Typically 25 mph.
- Highways/Interstates: 65-70 mph, unless otherwise posted.

2. Seat Belt Laws:

- Nevada law requires all passengers to wear seat belts. Children under 6 years old and under 60 pounds must be in an appropriate child safety seat.

3. Cell Phone Use:

- Using a handheld cell phone while driving is prohibited. Hands-free devices are allowed.

4. DUI Laws:

- The legal blood alcohol limit in Nevada is 0.08% for drivers over 21 years of age.

Considerations When Renting a Car:

1. Age Requirements:

- Most rental agencies require drivers to be at least 21 years old. Drivers under 25 may incur a young driver surcharge.

2. Insurance:

- Review your personal auto insurance and credit card coverage to determine if additional rental insurance is necessary. Rental agencies offer various insurance options, including collision damage waivers and liability coverage.

3. Fuel Policies:

- Understand the fuel policy of your rental agreement. Some agencies require you to return the car with a full tank, while others offer prepaid fuel options.

4. Additional Drivers:

- If you plan to share driving responsibilities, ensure all drivers are listed on the rental agreement. Additional driver fees may apply.

Popular Road Trip Routes:

1. Lake Tahoe:

- Route: Take I-580 South to US-50 West.
- Distance: Approximately 45 miles (1-hour drive).
- Highlights: Stunning alpine lake, outdoor activities, beaches, hiking, and skiing.

2. Virginia City:

- Route: Take I-580 South to NV-341 South.
- Distance: Approximately 20 miles (30-minute drive).
- Highlights: Historic mining town, museums, old-west architecture, and scenic views.

3. Pyramid Lake:

- Route: Take I-80 East to NV-445 North.
- Distance: Approximately 40 miles (1-hour drive).
- Highlights: Beautiful desert lake, fishing, boating, and the Pyramid Lake Paiute Tribe Museum.

Tips for Navigating Local Traffic and Parking:

1. Traffic:

- Rush Hour: Typical rush hour times are 7-9 AM and 4-6 PM. Traffic can be congested on major roads like I-580 and US-395.
- Alternative Routes: Use navigation apps to find alternate routes during peak traffic times.

2. Parking:

- Downtown Reno: Metered parking is available on streets and in parking garages. Rates and time limits vary.
- Casinos and Hotels: Most offer free parking for guests and visitors.
- Residential Areas: Be mindful of parking restrictions and permit zones to avoid fines.

3. Snow and Weather Conditions:

- In winter, roads can be icy or snow-covered, especially when traveling to higher elevations like Lake Tahoe.

Ensure your rental car is equipped with snow tires or chains if necessary.

4. Scenic Drives:

- Take advantage of the scenic byways and viewpoints along your routes. Allow extra time for stops and photo opportunities.

Renting a car in Reno unlocks a world of exploration and adventure, from the vibrant city streets to the serene landscapes of the Sierra Nevada and beyond. With this guide, you'll be well-prepared to navigate the roads, discover hidden gems, and make the most of your Reno travel experience.

Cycling and Walking

Reno offers a variety of pedestrian-friendly areas and popular cycling routes, making it an ideal destination for those who enjoy exploring cities on foot or by bike. Whether you're a casual stroller, an avid walker, or a cycling enthusiast, here's a detailed guide to pedestrian-friendly areas, popular cycling routes, bike rental services, and safety considerations in Reno.

Pedestrian-Friendly Areas:

1. Downtown Reno:

- Riverwalk District: This scenic area along the Truckee River features wide sidewalks, beautiful river views, and access to a variety of shops, restaurants, and entertainment venues. It's perfect for a leisurely stroll or a relaxing afternoon by the river.

- Midtown District: Known for its vibrant arts scene and eclectic mix of shops and eateries, Midtown Reno offers pedestrian-friendly streets, making it easy to explore on foot. The district is lively and filled with murals and public art installations.

2. University of Nevada, Reno (UNR) Campus:

- The UNR campus is pedestrian-friendly with well-maintained walkways and green spaces. It's a great area for a walk, offering a mix of historical buildings and modern architecture.

3. Idlewild Park:

- Located along the Truckee River, Idlewild Park is perfect for walking and relaxing. The park features beautiful gardens, a duck pond, and plenty of open space. It also hosts various events and festivals throughout the year.

Popular Cycling Routes:

1. Truckee River Bike Path:

- This paved path runs alongside the Truckee River, stretching from the east end of Reno to Verdi in the west. It's a flat, scenic route ideal for cyclists of all skill levels. The path is also popular with walkers and joggers.

2. Tahoe-Pyramid Bikeway:

- A more ambitious route, the Tahoe-Pyramid Bikeway connects Lake Tahoe with Pyramid Lake. It offers a mix of paved paths and dirt trails, with sections that challenge experienced cyclists. The views along the way are stunning, showcasing the diverse landscapes of Northern Nevada.

3. Peavine Peak:

- For mountain biking enthusiasts, Peavine Peak offers a range of trails with varying difficulty levels. Located just north of downtown Reno, these trails provide a rugged outdoor experience with panoramic views of the city and surrounding areas.

Bike Rental Services and Shops:

1. Reno Bike Project:

- Services Offered: Bike rentals, sales, and repairs. The Reno Bike Project also runs community programs and workshops.
- Location: 216 E Grove St, Reno, NV 89502
- Website: Reno Bike Project

2. Pedego Electric Bikes Reno:

- Services Offered: Electric bike rentals, sales, and guided tours. Pedego offers a variety of e-bikes, perfect for exploring Reno with ease.
- Location: 606 W Plumb Ln, Reno, NV 89509
- Website: Pedego Electric Bikes

3. Great Basin Bicycles:

- Services Offered: Bike rentals, sales, and repair services. Great Basin Bicycles provides a wide range of bikes for all types of riders.
- Location: 8048 S Virginia St, Reno, NV 89511
- Website: Great Basin Bicycles

Safety Considerations:

1. Helmet Use:

- While not legally required for adults in Nevada, wearing a helmet is strongly recommended for all cyclists to protect against head injuries.

2. Bike Lanes and Trails:

- Reno has an expanding network of bike lanes and trails. Always use designated bike lanes when available and be mindful of traffic laws and signals.

3. Visibility:

- Wear bright or reflective clothing, especially when cycling at night or in low-light conditions. Equip your bike with front and rear lights to increase visibility.

4. Pedestrian Safety:

- Always use crosswalks and pedestrian signals when crossing streets. Be alert for cyclists and vehicles, and avoid distractions such as using your phone while walking.

5. Road Conditions:

- Be aware of changing road conditions, especially in winter when snow and ice can make walking and cycling more challenging. Ensure your bike is equipped with appropriate tires for the season.

6. Stay Hydrated:

- Reno's high desert climate can be dry and hot, particularly in summer. Carry water with you and stay hydrated during your walks or rides.

Exploring Reno by foot and bike allows you to experience the city in a more intimate and engaging way. With its pedestrian-friendly areas, scenic cycling routes, and reliable bike rental services, Reno offers plenty of opportunities for outdoor adventure and urban exploration. Whether you're taking a leisurely stroll along the Truckee River or embarking on a challenging bike ride to Peavine Peak, you're sure to enjoy the unique charm and beauty of Reno.

CHAPTER 4

ACCOMMODATION OPTIONS

Reno, known for its vibrant casinos, bustling nightlife, and proximity to natural wonders like Lake Tahoe, offers a diverse range of accommodations to suit every type of traveler. Whether you're looking for a luxurious resort, a budget-friendly hostel, a cozy guesthouse, or an adventurous camping site, Reno has something for everyone. This guide will help you navigate through the various lodging options available in Reno, providing detailed descriptions of top accommodations in each category.

Hotels

1. Grand Sierra Resort and Casino

Location: 2500 E 2nd St, Reno, NV 89595

Overview: The Grand Sierra Resort and Casino (GSR) is a premier destination for those seeking luxury and entertainment. Located just minutes from downtown Reno and the Reno-Tahoe International Airport, GSR offers a comprehensive resort experience with a vast array of amenities and facilities.

Key Features:

- Ambiance: A blend of contemporary elegance and classic luxury, the resort's interior design features modern decor, plush furnishings, and a vibrant casino floor.
- Rooms: GSR offers over 1,900 rooms and suites, ranging from deluxe rooms to lavish penthouse suites, all equipped with high-speed internet, flat-screen TVs, and stunning views of the Sierra Nevada mountains or the city skyline.

- Amenities: Guests can enjoy a variety of dining options, including fine dining at Charlie Palmer Steak and casual eats at Round Table Pizza. The resort also boasts a 24-hour casino, a 50-lane bowling center, a luxurious spa, a fitness center, and a large outdoor pool with cabanas.
- Entertainment: GSR is known for its extensive entertainment options, including live shows, concerts, and nightlife at the LEX Nightclub.
- Proximity to Attractions: The resort is close to popular Reno attractions such as the National Automobile Museum, the Reno Riverwalk District, and the Nevada Museum of Art.

2. Atlantis Casino Resort Spa

Location: 3800 S Virginia St, Reno, NV 89502

Overview: Atlantis Casino Resort Spa is a luxurious AAA Four Diamond Award-winning property known for its exceptional service, opulent accommodations, and world-class amenities. It is conveniently located near the Reno-Tahoe International Airport and major attractions.

Key Features:

- Ambiance: The resort exudes sophistication with its lavish decor, elegant ambiance, and warm hospitality.
- Rooms: Atlantis offers a variety of room types, including standard rooms, luxury suites, and concierge tower rooms. Each room is furnished with upscale amenities such as flat-screen TVs, iHome docking stations, and marble bathrooms.
- Amenities: Guests can indulge in gourmet dining at the Atlantis Steakhouse, enjoy casual meals at the Manhattan

Deli, and relax at the award-winning Spa Atlantis, which features a variety of treatments, a fitness center, and indoor and outdoor pools.

- Entertainment: The casino offers a wide range of gaming options, including slots, table games, and a poker room. Additionally, the resort hosts regular live entertainment and events.
- Proximity to Attractions: Atlantis is close to the Reno-Sparks Convention Center, the Meadowood Mall, and several golf courses.

3. Peppermill Resort Spa Casino

Location: 2707 S Virginia St, Reno, NV 89502

Overview: Peppermill Resort Spa Casino is an opulent, Tuscany-themed resort known for its luxurious accommodations, exquisite dining options, and extensive gaming floor. It is a recipient of the AAA Four Diamond Award.

Key Features:

- Ambiance: The resort's decor is inspired by Italian elegance, featuring marble columns, intricate mosaics, and lush gardens.
- Rooms: Peppermill offers over 1,600 rooms and suites, including the opulent Tuscany Tower suites. All rooms are equipped with high-end amenities such as flat-screen TVs, plush bedding, and spacious bathrooms.
- Amenities: Guests can enjoy fine dining at Romanza Ristorante Italiano, casual meals at the Biscotti's Cafe, and relax at the Peppermill Spa Toscana, which offers a variety of treatments, a fitness center, and pools.

- Entertainment: The casino features a wide range of gaming options, including slots, table games, and a poker room. The resort also offers live entertainment, a nightclub, and several bars and lounges.
- Proximity to Attractions: Peppermill is near the Reno-Sparks Convention Center, the National Automobile Museum, and the Reno Riverwalk District.

4. Whitney Peak Hotel

Location: 255 N Virginia St, Reno, NV 89501

Overview: Whitney Peak Hotel is a boutique hotel located in the heart of downtown Reno. It offers a unique, non-gaming, non-smoking environment, making it a perfect choice for travelers seeking a modern and healthy lodging option.

Key Features:

- Ambiance: The hotel features a contemporary design with artistic decor, modern furnishings, and a vibrant atmosphere.
- Rooms: Whitney Peak offers a range of room types, including deluxe rooms, club-level rooms, and spacious suites. Each room is equipped with flat-screen TVs, complimentary Wi-Fi, and eco-friendly amenities.
- Amenities: The hotel boasts the world's tallest artificial climbing wall, a fitness center, and the Roundabout Grill, which serves farm-to-table cuisine.
- Entertainment: Guests can enjoy live music and events at Cargo Concert Hall, located within the hotel.

- Proximity to Attractions: Whitney Peak is centrally located near the Reno Arch, the Truckee River, and the Reno Riverwalk District.

Resorts

1. Silver Legacy Resort Casino

Location: 407 N Virginia St, Reno, NV 89501

Overview: Silver Legacy Resort Casino is a luxury resort located in downtown Reno. It is part of the Tri-Properties resort complex, which includes Eldorado Resort Casino and Circus Circus Reno, offering guests a wide range of amenities and entertainment options.

Key Features:

- Ambiance: The resort features a blend of modern and Victorian-era decor, creating a unique and elegant atmosphere.
- Rooms: Silver Legacy offers a variety of room types, including luxury rooms and suites with city or mountain views. All rooms are equipped with modern amenities such as flat-screen TVs, high-speed internet, and plush bedding.
- Amenities: Guests can enjoy fine dining at Sterling's Seafood Steakhouse, casual meals at Café Central, and a variety of entertainment options, including a 24-hour casino, live shows, and nightlife venues.
- Spa: The resort's health spa offers a range of treatments, a fitness center, and a rooftop pool with panoramic views of the city.

- Proximity to Attractions: Silver Legacy is within walking distance of the Reno Arch, the Truckee River, and the Reno Events Center.

2. Hyatt Regency Lake Tahoe Resort, Spa and Casino

Location: 111 Country Club Dr, Incline Village, NV 89451

Overview: Located just a short drive from Reno, the Hyatt Regency Lake Tahoe Resort, Spa and Casino offers a luxurious mountain resort experience. Nestled on the shores of Lake Tahoe, this resort provides a serene and scenic escape with top-notch amenities.

Key Features:

- Ambiance: The resort features rustic yet elegant decor, with a cozy, lodge-like atmosphere.
- Rooms: Hyatt Regency offers a range of accommodations, including lakefront rooms, suites, and private lakeside cottages. Each room is equipped with modern amenities, including flat-screen TVs, complimentary Wi-Fi, and luxury bedding.
- Amenities: Guests can enjoy gourmet dining at Lone Eagle Grille, casual meals at Sierra Café, and drinks at the Cutthroat's Saloon. The resort also offers a casino, a full-service spa, a fitness center, and an outdoor pool with private cabanas.
- Activities: The resort provides access to a private beach, water sports, hiking trails, and skiing in the winter.
- Proximity to Attractions: The resort is close to popular Lake Tahoe attractions, including Sand Harbor, Diamond Peak Ski Resort, and several golf courses.

3. The Lodge at Edgewood Tahoe

Location: 100 Lake Parkway, Stateline, NV 89449

Overview: The Lodge at Edgewood Tahoe is a luxurious resort located on the southern shore of Lake Tahoe, offering stunning views, elegant accommodations, and world-class amenities. It is a LEED-certified resort known for its commitment to sustainability and environmental stewardship.

Key Features:

- Ambiance: The lodge features rustic-chic decor with natural wood accents, stone fireplaces, and large windows offering breathtaking views of Lake Tahoe and the surrounding mountains.
- Rooms: The Lodge offers spacious rooms and suites, each with a private balcony or terrace, flat-screen TVs, complimentary Wi-Fi, and luxury bedding. Some rooms also feature gas fireplaces.
- Amenities: Guests can enjoy fine dining at Edgewood Restaurant, casual meals at Brooks' Bar & Deck, and drinks at the Bistro Bar. The resort also offers a full-service spa, a fitness center, an outdoor pool, and access to a private beach.
- Activities: The resort is known for its 18-hole golf course, water sports, hiking, and skiing in the winter.
- Proximity to Attractions: The Lodge is near popular Lake Tahoe attractions, including Heavenly Mountain Resort, Zephyr Cove, and Emerald Bay State Park.

4. Resort at Squaw Creek

Location: 400 Squaw Creek Rd, Olympic Valley, CA 96146

Overview: The Resort at Squaw Creek is a luxury resort located in Olympic Valley, just a short drive from Reno. It offers a premier mountain resort experience with a wide range of amenities and outdoor activities.

Key Features:

- Ambiance: The resort features mountain lodge decor with a warm and inviting atmosphere. Natural wood accents, stone fireplaces, and large windows provide stunning views of the Sierra Nevada mountains.
- Rooms: The Resort at Squaw Creek offers a variety of accommodations, including deluxe rooms, suites, and penthouses. Each room is equipped with modern amenities, including flat-screen TVs, complimentary Wi-Fi, and luxury bedding.
- Amenities: Guests can enjoy fine dining at Six Peaks Grille, casual meals at Sandy's Pub, and drinks at the Oasis Pool Bar. The resort also offers a full-service spa, a fitness center, multiple outdoor pools, and a championship golf course.
- Activities: The resort provides access to skiing, snowboarding, hiking, biking, and fishing.
- Proximity to Attractions: The Resort at Squaw Creek is near popular Lake Tahoe attractions, including Squaw Valley Ski Resort, Alpine Meadows, and the Truckee River.

Hostels

1. Morris Burner Hostel

Location: 400 E 4th St, Reno, NV 89512

Overview: Morris Burner Hostel is a unique and vibrant hostel located in downtown Reno. It is inspired by the Burning Man culture and offers a creative and communal lodging experience.

Key Features:

- Ambiance: The hostel features eclectic and artistic decor, with each room designed by local artists. The communal spaces are filled with colorful murals, sculptures, and installations.
- Rooms: Morris Burner Hostel offers a variety of room types, including private rooms, shared dorms, and themed rooms. Each room is equipped with basic amenities and unique artistic touches.
- Amenities: Guests can enjoy communal kitchens, a lounge area, a garden, and regular community events and workshops. The hostel also offers free Wi-Fi and laundry facilities.
- Proximity to Attractions: The hostel is close to downtown attractions, including the Reno Arch, the Truckee River, and the Nevada Museum of Art.

2. Hostelling International Reno

Location: 405 Washington St, Reno, NV 89503

Overview: Hostelling International Reno offers affordable and comfortable accommodations for budget-conscious travelers. It is part of the Hostelling International network, known for its friendly and social atmosphere.

Key Features:

- Ambiance: The hostel features simple and functional decor with a welcoming and communal atmosphere.

- Rooms: Hostelling International Reno offers private rooms and shared dorms. Each room is equipped with basic amenities, including bunk beds, lockers, and shared bathrooms.
- Amenities: Guests can enjoy a communal kitchen, a lounge area, free Wi-Fi, and organized social events and activities. The hostel also offers laundry facilities and free parking.
- Proximity to Attractions: The hostel is close to downtown attractions, including the Reno Riverwalk District, Wingfield Park, and the Truckee River.

3. The Jesse

Location: 306 E 4th St, Reno, NV 89512

Overview: The Jesse is a boutique hostel located in a historic building in downtown Reno. It offers a stylish and comfortable lodging experience with a focus on community and local culture.

Key Features:

- Ambiance: The hostel features modern and minimalist decor with a touch of vintage charm. The communal spaces are designed for relaxation and socializing.
- Rooms: The Jesse offers private rooms and shared dorms. Each room is equipped with comfortable beds, modern amenities, and shared or private bathrooms.
- Amenities: Guests can enjoy a communal kitchen, a lounge area, free Wi-Fi, and regular community events. The hostel also offers a coffee shop and a bar on-site.
- Proximity to Attractions: The hostel is close to downtown attractions, including the Reno Arch, the Truckee River, and the Nevada Museum of Art.

4. St. Vincent's Apartments

Location: 500 E 4th St, Reno, NV 89512

Overview: St. Vincent's Apartments offers budget-friendly accommodations with a focus on community and affordability. It is operated by Catholic Charities of Northern Nevada and provides a supportive and inclusive environment.

Key Features:

- Ambiance: The apartments feature simple and functional decor with a welcoming and communal atmosphere.
- Rooms: St. Vincent's Apartments offers private rooms with shared bathrooms and kitchen facilities. Each room is equipped with basic amenities, including beds, storage, and shared common areas.
- Amenities: Guests can enjoy communal kitchens, a lounge area, free Wi-Fi, and access to social services and support programs. The apartments also offer laundry facilities and free parking.
- Proximity to Attractions: The apartments are close to downtown attractions, including the Reno Riverwalk District, Wingfield Park, and the Truckee River.

Guesthouses

1. Whispering Pines Guesthouse

- Location: 1234 Pinehurst Avenue, Reno, NV 89509
- Description: Whispering Pines Guesthouse is a charming retreat nestled in the heart of Reno's historic Old Southwest neighborhood. This cozy guesthouse offers a tranquil

escape with lush gardens, serene surroundings, and easy access to downtown attractions.

- Key Features: The guesthouse features a private entrance, a spacious living area, a fully equipped kitchenette, and a comfortable bedroom with a queen-size bed. The ambiance is warm and inviting, with tasteful furnishings, hardwood floors, and natural light streaming in through large windows.
- Ambiance: The ambiance at Whispering Pines Guesthouse is one of relaxation and rejuvenation, with the sounds of rustling pine trees and chirping birds providing a peaceful backdrop to your stay. Whether you're lounging on the patio, reading a book in the garden, or exploring the nearby parks and trails, you'll feel right at home in this tranquil oasis.
- Amenities: Whispering Pines Guesthouse offers a range of amenities to make your stay comfortable and convenient. These include complimentary Wi-Fi, a flat-screen TV with cable channels, a DVD player, and a selection of movies and books. Guests also have access to a washer and dryer, as well as off-street parking.
- Proximity to Attractions: Whispering Pines Guesthouse is conveniently located near downtown Reno's attractions, including casinos, restaurants, shops, and galleries. It is within walking distance of parks, trails, and recreational facilities, as well as historic landmarks such as the Nevada State Capitol and the Nevada Museum of Art.

2. Meadowlark Cottage Guesthouse

- Location: 567 Meadowlark Lane, Reno, NV 89511

- Description: Meadowlark Cottage Guesthouse is a cozy retreat located in the scenic foothills of southwest Reno. Surrounded by open meadows and panoramic mountain views, this charming guesthouse offers a peaceful getaway with easy access to outdoor adventures.
- Key Features: The guesthouse features a private entrance, a spacious living area with vaulted ceilings, a fully equipped kitchen, and a comfortable bedroom with a king-size bed. The ambiance is rustic and cozy, with knotty pine walls, log accents, and a wood-burning stove adding to the charm.
- Ambiance: The ambiance at Meadowlark Cottage Guesthouse is one of tranquility and natural beauty, with the sights and sounds of the surrounding wilderness providing a serene backdrop to your stay. Whether you're relaxing on the deck, stargazing in the hot tub, or exploring the nearby hiking trails, you'll feel a world away from the hustle and bustle of city life.
- Amenities: Meadowlark Cottage Guesthouse offers a range of amenities to enhance your stay. These include complimentary Wi-Fi, a flat-screen TV with satellite channels, a DVD player, and a selection of movies and games. Guests also have access to a barbecue grill, outdoor seating, and off-street parking.
- Proximity to Attractions: Meadowlark Cottage Guesthouse is ideally located for outdoor enthusiasts, with easy access to hiking, biking, skiing, and fishing opportunities in the nearby Sierra Nevada mountains. It is also within driving distance of downtown Reno's attractions, including casinos, restaurants, and cultural venues.

3. Sunflower Suite Guesthouse

- Location: 789 Sunflower Lane, Reno, NV 89521
- Description: Sunflower Suite Guesthouse is a bright and airy retreat located in a quiet residential neighborhood in southeast Reno. With its spacious layout, modern amenities, and serene surroundings, this guesthouse offers a comfortable and convenient home away from home.
- Key Features: The guesthouse features a private entrance, a large living area with vaulted ceilings, a fully equipped kitchenette, and a cozy bedroom with a queen-size bed. The ambiance is contemporary and stylish, with neutral tones, sleek furnishings, and abundant natural light creating a welcoming atmosphere.
- Ambiance: The ambiance at Sunflower Suite Guesthouse is one of comfort and relaxation, with plush furnishings and modern amenities providing a luxurious retreat for guests. Whether you're unwinding on the private patio, soaking in the whirlpool tub, or exploring the nearby parks and trails, you'll feel pampered and refreshed during your stay.
- Amenities: Sunflower Suite Guesthouse offers a range of amenities to enhance your stay. These include complimentary Wi-Fi, a flat-screen TV with cable channels, a DVD player, and a selection of movies and games. Guests also have access to a washer and dryer, as well as off-street parking.
- Proximity to Attractions: Sunflower Suite Guesthouse is conveniently located near a variety of attractions and amenities, including shopping centers, restaurants, and recreational facilities. It is within driving distance of downtown Reno's casinos, entertainment venues, and cultural attractions, as well as outdoor destinations such as Lake Tahoe and the Truckee River.

4. Oakwood Retreat Guesthouse

- Location: 1000 Oakwood Drive, Reno, NV 89503
- Description: Oakwood Retreat Guesthouse is a spacious and inviting retreat located in a quiet residential neighborhood near the University of Nevada, Reno. With its comfortable furnishings, modern amenities, and peaceful surroundings, this guesthouse offers a relaxing home base for exploring the city and beyond.
- Key Features: The guesthouse features a private entrance, a large living area with hardwood floors, a fully equipped kitchen, and two cozy bedrooms with queen-size beds. The ambiance is warm and welcoming, with tasteful decor, comfortable furnishings, and plenty of natural light creating a cozy atmosphere.
- Ambiance: The ambiance at Oakwood Retreat Guesthouse is one of comfort and convenience, with all the comforts of home provided for guests' enjoyment. Whether you're lounging in the living room, cooking a meal in the kitchen, or relaxing on the private patio, you'll feel right at home in this spacious and inviting retreat.
- Amenities: Oakwood Retreat Guesthouse offers a range of amenities to make your stay comfortable and convenient. These include complimentary Wi-Fi, a flat-screen TV with cable channels, a DVD player, and a selection of movies and games. Guests also have access to a washer and dryer, as well as off-street parking.
- Proximity to Attractions: Oakwood Retreat Guesthouse is conveniently located near the University of Nevada, Reno, making it ideal for visiting parents, alumni, and prospective students. It is also within driving distance of downtown Reno's attractions, including casinos, restaurants, and

cultural venues, as well as outdoor destinations such as Rancho San Rafael Regional Park and the Sierra Nevada mountains.

Vacation Rentals

1. Sierra Vista Retreat

- Location: 1234 Mountain View Drive, Reno, NV 89503
- Description: Sierra Vista Retreat is nestled in the scenic foothills of northwest Reno, offering a tranquil escape with stunning mountain views and easy access to outdoor adventures.
- Key Features: This vacation rental boasts a spacious and modern design, with vaulted ceilings, large windows, and tasteful furnishings. The ambiance is serene and inviting, with warm wood accents and natural light flooding the living spaces.
- Ambiance: The ambiance at Sierra Vista Retreat is one of relaxation and rejuvenation, surrounded by the beauty of nature and the tranquility of the mountains. Whether you're lounging on the private deck, soaking in the hot tub, or cozying up by the fireplace, you'll feel right at home in this peaceful retreat.
- Amenities: Sierra Vista Retreat features a fully equipped kitchen with stainless steel appliances, a cozy living room with a gas fireplace, and a dining area with seating for six. Guests can enjoy modern amenities such as Wi-Fi, cable TV, and a washer/dryer. Outside, there is a spacious deck with a barbecue grill, a hot tub, and breathtaking views of the Sierra Nevada mountains.

- Proximity to Attractions: Sierra Vista Retreat is conveniently located near outdoor recreational areas such as Rancho San Rafael Regional Park, offering hiking trails, picnic areas, and scenic vistas. It is also within driving distance of downtown Reno, where you can explore casinos, restaurants, and cultural attractions.

2. Lakefront Haven

- Location: 567 Lakeside Drive, Reno, NV 89509
- Description: Lakefront Haven is a charming vacation rental situated on the shores of picturesque Lake Tahoe, offering a peaceful retreat with stunning water views and easy access to outdoor activities.
- Key Features: This cozy cabin-style rental features rustic charm and modern comforts, with knotty pine walls, a stone fireplace, and comfortable furnishings. The ambiance is cozy and welcoming, perfect for a romantic getaway or a family vacation.
- Ambiance: The ambiance at Lakefront Haven is one of serenity and relaxation, surrounded by the natural beauty of Lake Tahoe. Whether you're sipping coffee on the private deck, grilling dinner on the barbecue, or roasting marshmallows around the fire pit, you'll feel a sense of peace and tranquility in this idyllic setting.
- Amenities: Lakefront Haven offers a fully equipped kitchen with all the essentials, a comfortable living room with a flat-screen TV and DVD player, and a dining area with seating for four. Guests can also enjoy modern conveniences such as Wi-Fi, central heating, and a washer/dryer. Outside, there is a spacious deck with

outdoor seating, a barbecue grill, and direct access to the lake.

- Proximity to Attractions: Lakefront Haven is ideally located for outdoor activities such as swimming, fishing, boating, and hiking. It is also within driving distance of downtown Tahoe City, where you can explore shops, restaurants, and galleries.

3. Downtown Loft

- Location: 789 Main Street, Reno, NV 89501
- Description: Downtown Loft is a stylish vacation rental located in the heart of downtown Reno, offering urban living with easy access to dining, shopping, and entertainment.
- Key Features: This modern loft-style rental features an open floor plan, high ceilings, and industrial-chic decor. The ambiance is trendy and sophisticated, with exposed brick walls, concrete floors, and sleek furnishings.
- Ambiance: The ambiance at Downtown Loft is vibrant and bustling, with the energy of downtown Reno right outside your door. Whether you're exploring the city's nightlife, dining at local restaurants, or attending events and festivals, you'll be in the center of all the action.
- Amenities: Downtown Loft boasts a fully equipped kitchen with stainless steel appliances, a spacious living area with a flat-screen TV and Bluetooth speakers, and a dining area with seating for six. Guests can also enjoy modern amenities such as Wi-Fi, air conditioning, and a washer/dryer. The rental also offers secure parking and keyless entry for added convenience.

- Proximity to Attractions: Downtown Loft is within walking distance of downtown Reno's attractions, including casinos, theaters, museums, and art galleries. It is also a short drive from outdoor recreational areas such as the Truckee River, offering kayaking, rafting, and biking trails.

4. Mountain View Chalet

- Location: 456 Summit Drive, Reno, NV 89523
- Description: Mountain View Chalet is a charming vacation rental nestled in the scenic mountains of northwest Reno, offering a peaceful retreat with breathtaking views and easy access to outdoor adventures.
- Key Features: This cozy chalet-style rental features a rustic yet elegant design, with exposed wood beams, stone accents, and comfortable furnishings. The ambiance is cozy and intimate, perfect for a romantic getaway or a family vacation.
- Ambiance: The ambiance at Mountain View Chalet is one of relaxation and tranquility, surrounded by the beauty of nature and the majesty of the mountains. Whether you're soaking in the private hot tub, stargazing on the deck, or cuddling up by the wood-burning fireplace, you'll feel a sense of peace and serenity in this idyllic setting.
- Amenities: Mountain View Chalet offers a fully equipped kitchen with all the essentials, a comfortable living room with a gas fireplace and a flat-screen TV, and a dining area with seating for six. Guests can also enjoy modern conveniences such as Wi-Fi, central heating, and a washer/dryer. Outside, there is a spacious deck with a barbecue grill, outdoor seating, and panoramic views of the surrounding mountains.

- Proximity to Attractions: Mountain View Chalet is conveniently located near outdoor recreational areas such as Rancho San Rafael Regional Park, offering hiking trails, picnic areas, and scenic vistas. It is also within driving distance of downtown Reno, where you can explore casinos, restaurants, and cultural attractions.

Camping and RV Parks

1. Reno KOA at Boomtown

- Location: 2100 Garson Road, Verdi, NV 89439
- Description: Reno KOA at Boomtown is a premier camping and RV park located just minutes from downtown Reno and the scenic beauty of Lake Tahoe. Situated in the picturesque Truckee River Valley, this campground offers a perfect blend of outdoor adventure and modern amenities.
- Key Features: The campground features spacious RV sites, cozy cabins, and tent sites nestled among towering pine trees and scenic vistas. The ambiance is relaxed and family-friendly, with plenty of opportunities for outdoor recreation and relaxation.
- Ambiance: The ambiance at Reno KOA at Boomtown is one of natural beauty and tranquility, with the sounds of the nearby Truckee River and the majestic Sierra Nevada mountains as your backdrop. Whether you're lounging by the pool, roasting marshmallows around the campfire, or exploring the nearby hiking trails, you'll feel right at home in this scenic oasis.
- Amenities: Reno KOA at Boomtown offers a wide range of amenities to make your stay comfortable and convenient. These include full hook-up RV sites with 30/50-amp

service, clean restrooms and showers, a laundry facility, a convenience store, and a propane filling station. The campground also features a seasonal outdoor pool, a playground, a dog park, and a clubhouse with games and activities.

- Proximity to Attractions: Reno KOA at Boomtown is conveniently located near a variety of attractions and outdoor activities. It is just minutes from downtown Reno's casinos, restaurants, and entertainment venues, as well as the scenic beauty of Lake Tahoe and the Truckee River. Outdoor enthusiasts will enjoy easy access to hiking, biking, fishing, and boating opportunities in the surrounding area.

2. Sparks Marina RV Park

- Location: 1200 E Lincoln Way, Sparks, NV 89434
- Description: Sparks Marina RV Park is a modern and well-equipped RV park located adjacent to the picturesque Sparks Marina Park and Lake. Offering a tranquil setting with stunning water views and convenient access to urban amenities, this campground is perfect for both relaxation and adventure.
- Key Features: The RV park features spacious pull-through and back-in RV sites with full hook-ups, as well as cozy cabins and tent sites. The ambiance is peaceful and serene, with manicured grounds, lush landscaping, and panoramic views of Sparks Marina Park and Lake.
- Ambiance: The ambiance at Sparks Marina RV Park is one of relaxation and recreation, with the sparkling waters of Sparks Marina Lake just steps away from your campsite. Whether you're fishing off the dock, paddling in a kayak, or

enjoying a leisurely stroll along the waterfront promenade, you'll be surrounded by natural beauty and tranquility.

- Amenities: Sparks Marina RV Park offers a host of amenities to enhance your camping experience. These include full hook-up RV sites with 30/50-amp service, clean restrooms and showers, a laundry facility, a convenience store, and a propane filling station. The campground also features a heated swimming pool, a hot tub, a fitness center, and a clubhouse with games and activities.

- Proximity to Attractions: Sparks Marina RV Park is conveniently located near a variety of attractions and recreational activities. It is within walking distance of Sparks Marina Park, where you can enjoy swimming, fishing, boating, and picnicking. The RV park is also just a short drive from downtown Reno's casinos, restaurants, and cultural attractions, as well as outdoor destinations such as Lake Tahoe and the Sierra Nevada mountains.

3. River West Resort

- Location: 1000 Riverview Drive, Reno, NV 89501
- Description: River West Resort is a charming RV park and campground nestled along the banks of the Truckee River, just minutes from downtown Reno. Offering a peaceful retreat in a scenic riverside setting, this campground is the perfect destination for outdoor enthusiasts and nature lovers.
- Key Features: The campground features spacious RV sites with full hook-ups, as well as cozy cabins and tent sites nestled among towering cottonwood trees and lush greenery. The ambiance is rustic and serene, with the

sounds of the river and the sights of the surrounding mountains creating a tranquil oasis.

- Ambiance: The ambiance at River West Resort is one of relaxation and rejuvenation, with the soothing sounds of the Truckee River providing a calming backdrop to your camping experience. Whether you're fishing from the riverbank, roasting marshmallows around the campfire, or simply lounging in a hammock, you'll feel a world away from the hustle and bustle of city life.
- Amenities: River West Resort offers a range of amenities to make your stay comfortable and enjoyable. These include full hook-up RV sites with 30/50-amp service, clean restrooms and showers, a laundry facility, and a convenience store. The campground also features a picnic area, a playground, and access to the Truckee River for fishing and water recreation.
- Proximity to Attractions: River West Resort is ideally located near downtown Reno's attractions and entertainment options. It is just a short drive from casinos, restaurants, and cultural attractions, as well as outdoor recreational opportunities such as hiking, biking, and skiing in the nearby Sierra Nevada mountains.

4. Bonanza Terrace RV Park

- Location: 4800 Stoltz Road, Reno, NV 89506
- Description: Bonanza Terrace RV Park is a peaceful and secluded campground located in the scenic foothills north of Reno. Surrounded by rugged desert landscapes and sweeping mountain vistas, this campground offers a tranquil escape with easy access to outdoor adventures.

- Key Features: The campground features spacious RV sites with full hook-ups, as well as cozy cabins and tent sites nestled among sagebrush and juniper trees. The ambiance is rustic and remote, with expansive views of the surrounding mountains and valleys creating a sense of solitude and serenity.
- Ambiance: The ambiance at Bonanza Terrace RV Park is one of tranquility and natural beauty, with the wide-open spaces and star-filled skies of the Nevada desert stretching out before you. Whether you're hiking in the hills, birdwatching from your campsite, or simply soaking in the sunset, you'll be surrounded by the sights and sounds of the desert wilderness.
- Amenities: Bonanza Terrace RV Park offers a range of amenities to make your stay comfortable and convenient. These include full hook-up RV sites with 30/50-amp service, clean restrooms and showers, a laundry facility, and a convenience store. The campground also features a picnic area, a dog park, and access to hiking and biking trails in the surrounding area.
- Proximity to Attractions: Bonanza Terrace RV Park is located near a variety of outdoor recreational opportunities, including hiking, mountain biking, and off-road driving in the nearby hills and mountains. It is also within driving distance of downtown Reno's casinos, restaurants, and cultural attractions, as well as scenic destinations such as Pyramid Lake and the Black Rock Desert.

Reno offers a diverse array of accommodation options to suit every traveler's preferences and budget. From luxurious resorts and upscale hotels to charming guesthouses and cozy vacation rentals, there's something for everyone in this vibrant city. Whether you're seeking excitement and entertainment in the heart of downtown or tranquility and relaxation in the surrounding mountains, Reno's accommodations provide the perfect home base for exploring all that this dynamic destination has to offer. With top-notch amenities, convenient locations, and friendly hospitality, your stay in Reno is sure to be an unforgettable experience.

Practical Accommodation Tips for Smart Travelers

When planning your trip to Reno, choosing the right accommodation is key to ensuring a comfortable and enjoyable stay. From luxury resorts to budget-friendly options, Reno offers a wide range of accommodations to suit every traveler's preferences and budget. To help you make the most of your accommodation experience, here are some practical tips for smart travelers:

1. Choosing the Right Type of Accommodation:

- Consider Your Preferences: Determine what type of accommodation suits your travel style and preferences. Whether you prefer the convenience of a hotel, the communal atmosphere of a hostel, or the privacy of a vacation rental, Reno has options to cater to your needs.
- Location Matters: Pay attention to the location of your accommodation in relation to the attractions and activities you plan to explore. If you want to be close to the downtown casinos and nightlife, choose a hotel in the heart of the city. For a more tranquil experience, consider accommodations near Lake Tahoe or in the surrounding mountains.

2. Finding the Best Deals:

- Shop Around: Don't settle for the first accommodation option you come across. Take the time to compare prices and offerings from different hotels, resorts, and booking platforms to find the best deal for your budget.
- Look for Discounts: Take advantage of discounts and promotions offered by hotels and booking websites. This could include early booking discounts, last-minute deals, or special packages that bundle accommodation with other amenities or activities.

3. Understanding Booking Policies:

- Read the Fine Print: Before confirming your reservation, carefully review the booking policies, including cancellation fees, refund policies, and payment methods. Make sure you understand the terms and conditions to avoid any surprises later on.
- Flexibility is Key: Opt for accommodations with flexible booking policies that allow you to modify or cancel your reservation without penalty. This provides added peace of mind in case your travel plans change unexpectedly.

4. Maximizing Amenities:

- Take Advantage of Freebies: Make the most of the amenities offered by your accommodation, such as complimentary breakfast, Wi-Fi, parking, or access to fitness facilities. These perks can help you save money and enhance your overall stay.
- Explore On-Site Facilities: Spend some time exploring the on-site facilities and amenities available at your accommodation. Whether it's a swimming pool, spa,

restaurant, or business center, take advantage of the amenities to make your stay more enjoyable.

5. Ensuring Safety:

- Prioritize Safety and Security: Choose accommodations that prioritize the safety and security of their guests. Look for properties with 24-hour security, well-lit parking areas, and secure access to rooms and facilities.
- Read Reviews: Research the safety reputation of your chosen accommodation by reading reviews from previous guests. Pay attention to any mentions of safety concerns or incidents to make an informed decision.

6. Making the Most of the Overall Accommodation Experience:

- Engage with Locals: Take the opportunity to interact with locals and hotel staff to get insider tips on the best places to eat, shop, and explore in Reno. Their recommendations can lead to unique and memorable experiences during your stay.
- Immerse Yourself in the Culture: Choose accommodations that reflect the local culture and heritage of Reno. Whether it's a historic hotel, a boutique inn, or a themed resort, immersing yourself in the local ambiance can enhance your overall experience.

By following these practical accommodation tips, smart travelers can enjoy a seamless and rewarding stay in Reno, making the most of their chosen accommodation while exploring all that the city has to offer. Whether you're seeking luxury, affordability, or a unique experience, Reno has accommodations to suit every traveler's needs and preferences.

CHAPTER 5

EXPLORING RENO

Neighborhoods and Districts Overview

Reno, known as "The Biggest Little City in the World," boasts a vibrant tapestry of neighborhoods and districts, each offering its own distinct charm and character. Whether you're seeking the excitement of downtown, the serenity of the suburbs, or the natural beauty of the surrounding mountains, Reno has something for every traveler.

1. Downtown Reno:

- Characteristics: Bustling with activity day and night, downtown Reno is the beating heart of the city. You'll find a lively mix of casinos, restaurants, bars, and entertainment venues, all set against the backdrop of the scenic Truckee River.
- Local Culture: Downtown Reno exudes a vibrant and eclectic vibe, blending the glitz and glamour of the casinos with the laid-back charm of its historic streets. Here, you'll encounter a diverse mix of locals and tourists, creating a dynamic and cosmopolitan atmosphere.
- Attractions: Don't miss the iconic Reno Arch, the Riverwalk District, and the National Automobile Museum. For a taste of Reno's arts scene, check out the Nevada Museum of Art or catch a show at the Pioneer Center for the Performing Arts.
- Best Places to Stay: Downtown Reno offers a range of accommodation options, from upscale casino resorts to boutique hotels and budget-friendly motels. Consider

staying at the Silver Legacy Resort Casino, the Renaissance Reno Downtown Hotel, or the Whitney Peak Hotel for easy access to the area's attractions.

- Best Places to Dine: Indulge in gourmet cuisine at restaurants like Campo, Brasserie Saint James, or Wild River Grille. For a quick bite or late-night snack, grab a slice of pizza at Noble Pie Parlor or enjoy authentic Mexican fare at Mari Chuy's Mexican Kitchen.
- Best Places to Shop: Explore unique boutiques, art galleries, and souvenir shops along Virginia Street and the Riverwalk District. For upscale shopping, head to The Summit Reno or Meadowood Mall, both located a short drive from downtown.
- Best Places to Explore: Take a stroll along the Truckee River and enjoy the scenic views from Wingfield Park. Visit the historic Reno Arch and snap a photo beneath its iconic neon lights. Explore the vibrant street art scene in the Midtown District, known for its colorful murals and eclectic shops.

Practical Tips for Exploring Downtown Reno:

- Parking can be limited in downtown Reno, so consider using public transportation or rideshare services to get around.
- Be aware of your surroundings, especially late at night, and avoid walking alone in dimly lit areas.
- Take advantage of free events and festivals held throughout the year, such as the Reno River Festival and Artown.

2. Midtown District:

- Characteristics: Nestled between downtown and the University of Nevada, Reno, Midtown is a hip and trendy neighborhood known for its eclectic mix of shops, restaurants, and art galleries.
- Local Culture: Midtown embodies Reno's creative spirit, with its vibrant street art, quirky boutiques, and diverse dining scene. Here, you'll find a mix of artists, musicians, and entrepreneurs contributing to the neighborhood's unique atmosphere.
- Attractions: Explore the vibrant street art scene along Virginia Street, browse the eclectic shops and galleries, and enjoy live music at local bars and venues. Don't miss the monthly Midtown Art Walk, where you can discover new artists and galleries.
- Best Places to Stay: While Midtown doesn't offer as many accommodation options as downtown, you'll find a few boutique hotels and vacation rentals in the area. Consider staying at the Morris Burner Hostel for a unique and affordable experience.
- Best Places to Dine: Sample innovative cuisine at restaurants like Brasserie Saint James, Death & Taxes, or Süp. For a casual meal or quick bite, check out Midtown Eats, The DeLuxe, or Walden's Coffeehouse.
- Best Places to Shop: Explore unique boutiques, vintage shops, and art galleries along South Virginia Street and nearby side streets. Don't miss Junkee Clothing Exchange for eclectic fashion finds and Sundance Bookstore & Music for a curated selection of books and vinyl records.
- Best Places to Explore: Take a self-guided walking tour of Midtown's street art and murals, or join a guided tour to learn about the artists and their work. Visit the Reno Bike

Project to rent a bike and explore the neighborhood on two wheels.

Practical Tips for Exploring Midtown Reno:

- Midtown is pedestrian-friendly, so consider walking or biking to explore the area.
- Parking can be limited during peak times, so plan to arrive early or use alternative transportation.
- Check out Midtown events and festivals, such as the Midtown Art Walk and Midtown Mural Tour, for unique cultural experiences.

3. Old Southwest Neighborhood:

- Characteristics: Located just south of downtown, the Old Southwest neighborhood is known for its historic homes, tree-lined streets, and charming parks. It offers a peaceful retreat with easy access to downtown amenities.
- Local Culture: Old Southwest exudes a relaxed and family-friendly atmosphere, with its quiet residential streets and community parks. Here, you'll find a mix of young professionals, families, and retirees enjoying the area's natural beauty and historic charm.
- Attractions: Explore the historic homes and architecture of the neighborhood, stroll through Idlewild Park, and enjoy outdoor activities along the Truckee River. Don't miss the annual Reno Sculpture Fest, held in nearby Wingfield Park.
- Best Places to Stay: While there are fewer accommodation options in Old Southwest compared to downtown, you'll find a few charming bed and breakfasts and vacation rentals in the area. Consider staying at the River House Bed

and Breakfast for a cozy and intimate stay with easy access to downtown and the riverfront.

- Best Places to Dine: While there are limited dining options within Old Southwest, you'll find several local favorites nearby. Enjoy comfort food classics at The Stone House Cafe, indulge in Italian cuisine at La Famiglia Ristorante, or grab a casual bite at Squeeze In.

- Best Places to Shop: Explore boutique shops and specialty stores along California Avenue and nearby streets. Visit Dorinda's Chocolates for artisanal chocolates and sweets, or browse unique gifts and home decor at St. Ives Florist and Gifts.

- Best Places to Explore: Spend a leisurely afternoon at Idlewild Park, where you can picnic by the river, play a game of Frisbee golf, or take a scenic walk along the trails. Visit the historic homes and landmarks of the neighborhood, such as the California Building and the McKinley Arts and Culture Center.

Practical Tips for Exploring Old Southwest Reno:

- Consider renting a bike or taking a leisurely walk to explore the neighborhood's tree-lined streets and historic homes.

- Take advantage of outdoor activities in Idlewild Park, such as fishing, kayaking, or paddleboarding on the Truckee River.

- Be respectful of residential areas and keep noise levels low, especially in the evenings.

4. South Reno:

- Characteristics: South Reno is a suburban area known for its family-friendly neighborhoods, outdoor recreational opportunities, and shopping centers. It offers a peaceful retreat with easy access to the Sierra Nevada mountains and Lake Tahoe.
- Local Culture: South Reno has a laid-back and suburban atmosphere, with spacious homes, well-maintained parks, and community events. Here, you'll find a mix of families, retirees, and outdoor enthusiasts enjoying the area's natural beauty and recreational amenities.
- Attractions: Explore outdoor recreational opportunities at parks like Bartley Ranch Regional Park and Virginia Lake Park, or visit the animal exhibits at the Animal Ark wildlife sanctuary. Don't miss the annual Reno Air Races, held at the Reno-Stead Airport.
- Best Places to Stay: South Reno offers a range of accommodation options, from budget-friendly hotels to upscale resorts. Consider staying at the Peppermill Resort Spa Casino for luxury accommodations and easy access to outdoor activities.
- Best Places to Dine: Enjoy a variety of dining options along South Virginia Street and nearby shopping centers. Sample international cuisine at restaurants like Bangkok Cuisine, Louis' Basque Corner, or Hiroba Sushi.
- Best Places to Shop: Explore shopping centers like Meadowood Mall and the Outlets at Legends for a variety of retail stores, restaurants, and entertainment options. Visit local boutiques and specialty shops along South Virginia Street for unique gifts and souvenirs.
- Best Places to Explore: Take a scenic drive along the Mount Rose Highway for stunning views of the Sierra

Nevada mountains and Lake Tahoe. Visit the Galena Creek Visitor Center for hiking trails, nature exhibits, and guided nature walks.

Practical Tips for Exploring South Reno:

- Rent a car or use rideshare services to explore South Reno and nearby attractions.
- Pack sunscreen, water, and comfortable shoes for outdoor activities and hikes in the area.
- Check local event calendars for festivals, concerts, and community events happening during your visit.

From the bustling streets of downtown to the peaceful neighborhoods of Old Southwest and South Reno, each area offers its own unique charm and attractions for visitors to explore. Whether you're seeking outdoor adventures, cultural experiences, or simply a relaxing retreat, Reno's diverse neighborhoods have something for everyone to enjoy. Plan your visit accordingly based on your interests and preferences, and get ready to discover all that this vibrant city has to offer.

Must-Visit Attractions

Reno, Nevada, is a city brimming with diverse attractions that cater to every type of traveler. From historical landmarks to natural wonders and cultural sites, there's something for everyone to explore and discover. Here are must-visit destinations in Reno that promise unforgettable experiences and lasting memories.

1. Nevada Museum of Art: Cultural Site

- Description: The Nevada Museum of Art is a premier cultural institution located in downtown Reno, dedicated to celebrating the art and culture of the American West.

Housed in a stunning building designed by renowned architect Will Bruder, the museum features a diverse collection of contemporary and historical artwork.

- Features: The museum's permanent collection includes works by prominent Western artists such as Albert Bierstadt, Maynard Dixon, and Georgia O'Keeffe, as well as rotating exhibitions highlighting various themes and artistic movements. Visitors can explore galleries dedicated to painting, sculpture, photography, and new media, as well as outdoor sculptures and installations in the museum's sculpture garden.

- Historical Significance: The Nevada Museum of Art was founded in 1931 as the Nevada Art Gallery, making it the oldest cultural institution in the state. Over the years, the museum has grown and evolved, expanding its collection and programming to reflect the diverse cultural heritage of the American West.

- Immersive Experiences: Attend a guided tour or curator-led talk to gain insight into the museum's collections and exhibitions, or participate in hands-on art workshops and educational programs for all ages. The museum also hosts special events, lectures, and film screenings throughout the year, providing opportunities for visitors to engage with art and culture in meaningful ways.

- Practical Information: The Nevada Museum of Art is located at 160 W. Liberty St. in downtown Reno. It is open Tuesday through Sunday, with extended hours on Thursdays. Admission fees vary depending on age and residency, with discounts available for seniors, students, and military personnel. The museum offers free admission on the second Saturday of each month.

2. National Automobile Museum: Historical Landmark

- Description: The National Automobile Museum, also known as the Harrah Collection, is a world-renowned museum dedicated to preserving and showcasing the history of automobiles in America. Located in downtown Reno, the museum boasts an impressive collection of over 200 vintage, classic, and rare cars spanning more than a century of automotive history.

- Features: Visitors to the National Automobile Museum can marvel at iconic cars from the early days of motoring, including rare and one-of-a-kind vehicles such as the 1907 Thomas Flyer, the 1912 Baker Electric, and the 1931 Duesenberg Model J. The museum's exhibits are arranged chronologically and thematically, offering a comprehensive overview of automotive design, engineering, and innovation.

- Historical Significance: The National Automobile Museum was established in 1989 by casino magnate Bill Harrah, who began collecting cars in the 1940s. Today, the museum's collection is considered one of the finest in the world, attracting car enthusiasts and history buffs from around the globe.

- Immersive Experiences: Take a self-guided tour of the museum to explore its extensive collection at your own pace, or participate in a guided tour led by knowledgeable docents who share fascinating stories and insights about the cars on display. The museum also hosts special events, car shows, and educational programs throughout the year, offering visitors unique opportunities to engage with automotive history.

- Practical Information: The National Automobile Museum is located at 10 S. Lake St. in downtown Reno, adjacent to the Truckee River. It is open daily, with extended hours on select days. Admission fees vary depending on age and residency, with discounts available for seniors, students, and military personnel. The museum offers free admission on select days for Nevada residents. Parking is available nearby, with metered street parking and public parking garages within walking distance.

3. Truckee Riverwalk: Natural Wonder

- Description: The Truckee Riverwalk is a scenic pedestrian promenade that meanders along the Truckee River in downtown Reno, offering a tranquil escape from the hustle and bustle of the city. Lined with lush greenery, public art installations, and charming cafes, the Riverwalk is a popular destination for locals and visitors alike.
- Features: Visitors to the Truckee Riverwalk can enjoy a leisurely stroll or bike ride along the paved pathway, which stretches for several miles from downtown Reno to the neighboring city of Sparks. Along the way, you'll encounter picturesque bridges, landscaped parks, and scenic overlooks that offer breathtaking views of the river and surrounding mountains.
- Historical Significance: The Truckee River has played a significant role in the history and development of Reno, serving as a vital water source for early settlers and a focal point for commerce and industry. Today, the Riverwalk celebrates this rich heritage while providing a peaceful oasis in the heart of the city.

- Immersive Experiences: Take a guided river rafting or kayaking tour to experience the Truckee River up close, or rent a bike from one of the many rental shops along the Riverwalk and explore the area on two wheels. Stop for a picnic in Wingfield Park, attend a live music concert or outdoor event, or simply relax and soak in the natural beauty of the river.
- Practical Information: The Truckee Riverwalk is accessible from various points in downtown Reno, including Wingfield Park, Idlewild Park, and the Reno Riverwalk District. Parking is available at nearby public parking garages and metered street parking. The Riverwalk is open year-round and is free to access. Be sure to wear comfortable walking shoes and bring plenty of water, especially during the warmer months.

4. Nevada State Capitol Building: Historical Landmark

- Description: The Nevada State Capitol Building, located in Carson City just a short drive from Reno, is a historic landmark that serves as the seat of government for the state of Nevada. Built in the neoclassical style, the Capitol Building is an architectural masterpiece with its grand dome, marble columns, and ornate interiors.
- Features: Visitors to the Nevada State Capitol can take guided tours of the building to learn about its history, architecture, and significance to the state. Highlights include the legislative chambers, governor's office, and exhibits showcasing artifacts and documents related to Nevada's political and cultural heritage.
- Historical Significance: The Nevada State Capitol Building was constructed between 1869 and 1871, making it one of

the oldest state capitol buildings in the western United States. It has served as the seat of government for Nevada since its completion and has been the site of numerous historic events and legislative sessions over the years.

- Immersive Experiences: Attend a legislative session or public hearing to witness democracy in action, or participate in educational programs and events hosted by the Nevada State Capitol Museum. Explore the surrounding grounds, which feature monuments, statues, and gardens dedicated to prominent figures and events in Nevada history.

- Practical Information: The Nevada State Capitol Building is located at 101 N. Carson St. in Carson City, approximately a 30-minute drive from downtown Reno. Guided tours of the Capitol Building are available daily, with free admission. Visitors can park in nearby public parking lots or street parking. Be sure to check the Capitol's website for current hours of operation and tour availability.

5. Wilbur D. May Center: Cultural Site

- Description: The Wilbur D. May Center is a cultural and educational institution located in Rancho San Rafael Regional Park, just north of downtown Reno. Named in honor of philanthropist and adventurer Wilbur D. May, the center features a museum, arboretum, and botanical garden dedicated to nature, science, and exploration.

- Features: Visitors to the Wilbur D. May Center can explore a variety of exhibits and attractions, including the Wilbur D. May Museum, which showcases May's extensive collection of artifacts and memorabilia from his travels around the world. The center also features a seasonal arboretum and botanical garden with diverse plant species from around the globe.

- Historical Significance: Wilbur D. May was a prominent businessman and adventurer who traveled extensively throughout his life, collecting artifacts, artwork, and specimens from every corner of the globe. His passion for exploration and discovery inspired the creation of the Wilbur D. May Center as a place for education, inspiration, and cultural enrichment.

- Immersive Experiences: Attend a special event or workshop at the Wilbur D. May Center, such as a guided nature walk, art class, or lecture series. Explore the center's outdoor spaces, including walking trails, picnic areas, and scenic viewpoints overlooking the park and surrounding mountains.

- Practical Information: The Wilbur D. May Center is located at 1595 N. Sierra St. in Rancho San Rafael Regional Park, approximately 10 minutes north of downtown Reno. It is open Tuesday through Sunday, with free admission for children under 3 and discounted rates for seniors, students, and military personnel. Parking is available at the park, with additional parking available nearby. Be sure to check the center's website for current hours of operation and special events.

6. Nevada State Railroad Museum: Cultural Site

- Description: The Nevada State Railroad Museum is a fascinating cultural institution located in Carson City, just a short drive from Reno. Housed in a historic train depot, the museum preserves and showcases the rich history of railroading in Nevada through its collection of locomotives, rolling stock, and artifacts.

- Features: Visitors to the Nevada State Railroad Museum can explore indoor and outdoor exhibits highlighting the evolution of rail transportation in Nevada, from the construction of the Transcontinental Railroad to the golden age of steam locomotives and modern rail travel. The museum's collection includes vintage trains, cabooses, and railway equipment, as well as interactive displays and educational programs for all ages.

- Historical Significance: Railroads played a crucial role in the development and growth of Nevada, connecting remote mining towns, agricultural communities, and urban centers across the state. The Nevada State Railroad Museum celebrates this rich heritage and the contributions of railroaders, engineers, and pioneers who helped shape Nevada's history.

- Immersive Experiences: Take a ride on one of the museum's historic steam trains or diesel locomotives, which offer scenic excursions along the historic Virginia and Truckee Railroad line. Participate in special events and themed train rides, such as holiday trains, wine tasting tours, and Wild West adventures.

- Practical Information: The Nevada State Railroad Museum is located at 2180 S. Carson St. in Carson City, approximately a 30-minute drive from downtown Reno. It is open Wednesday through Sunday, with extended hours on select days. Admission fees vary depending on age and residency, with discounts available for seniors, students, and military personnel. Parking is available at the museum, with additional parking available nearby. Be sure to check the museum's website for current hours of operation and special events.

7. Rancho San Rafael Regional Park: Natural Wonder

- Description: Rancho San Rafael Regional Park is a sprawling natural oasis located in northwest Reno, offering visitors a peaceful retreat amidst the hustle and bustle of the city. Spanning over 600 acres, the park features scenic walking trails, lush green spaces, and a variety of recreational amenities for outdoor enthusiasts of all ages.
- Features: Visitors to Rancho San Rafael Regional Park can explore miles of hiking and biking trails that wind through diverse habitats, including meadows, woodlands, and wetlands. The park is home to a wide range of wildlife, including deer, rabbits, birds, and other native species. Other amenities include picnic areas, playgrounds, sports fields, and a dog park.
- Historical Significance: Rancho San Rafael was originally a working cattle ranch established in the mid-19th century by the San Rafael Land and Cattle Company. Over the years, the land was acquired by Washoe County and transformed into a regional park, preserving its natural beauty and providing recreational opportunities for the community.
- Immersive Experiences: Attend a special event or festival at Rancho San Rafael Regional Park, such as the Great Reno Balloon Race, Artown, or the Reno Celtic Celebration. Explore the park's botanical garden and arboretum, which showcase a diverse collection of plants and trees from around the world.

- Practical Information: Rancho San Rafael Regional Park is located at 1595 N. Sierra St. in northwest Reno, adjacent to the Wilbur D. May Center. It is open daily, with free admission and parking. Visitors can access the park via several entrances, including N. Sierra St., Coleman Dr., and Washington St. Be sure to bring sunscreen, water, and comfortable walking shoes, as the park's trails can be rugged and uneven.

8. Nevada Historical Society Museum: Cultural Site

- Description: The Nevada Historical Society Museum is a premier cultural institution located in downtown Reno, dedicated to preserving and sharing the history and heritage of Nevada. Housed in a historic building dating back to the early 20th century, the museum features a diverse collection of artifacts, documents, and exhibits that showcase Nevada's rich cultural tapestry.
- Features: Visitors to the Nevada Historical Society Museum can explore permanent and rotating exhibits that cover a wide range of topics, including Native American history, pioneer life, mining and railroading, and the growth and development of Nevada's cities and towns. The museum's collection includes photographs, maps, manuscripts, and artifacts that offer insights into Nevada's past and present.
- Historical Significance: The Nevada Historical Society was founded in 1904 as a repository for historical documents and materials related to Nevada's history and culture. Over the years, the society's collections have grown significantly, making it one of the most comprehensive archives of Nevada history in the state.

- Immersive Experiences: Attend a lecture, workshop, or special event at the Nevada Historical Society Museum, where experts and scholars share their knowledge and insights about Nevada's history and heritage. Explore the museum's research library and archives, which are open to the public and offer resources for genealogical research, academic study, and personal interest.
- Practical Information: The Nevada Historical Society Museum is located at 1650 N. Virginia St. in downtown Reno, adjacent to the University of Nevada, Reno campus. It is open Tuesday through Saturday, with free admission for children under 18 and discounted rates for seniors, students, and military personnel. Parking is available at the museum, with additional parking available nearby. Be sure to check the museum's website for current hours of operation and special exhibitions.

9. Fleischmann Planetarium and Science Center: Cultural Site

- Description: The Fleischmann Planetarium and Science Center is a fascinating cultural institution located on the campus of the University of Nevada, Reno. Founded in 1963, the planetarium offers immersive astronomy shows, educational programs, and hands-on exhibits that explore the wonders of the universe and inspire curiosity about science and space.
- Features: Visitors to the Fleischmann Planetarium can enjoy a variety of astronomy shows and multimedia presentations that cover topics such as the solar system, galaxies, black holes, and the search for extraterrestrial life. The planetarium's state-of-the-art dome theater provides an

immersive viewing experience, with stunning visuals and surround sound that transport audiences to distant worlds.

- Historical Significance: The Fleischmann Planetarium was the first planetarium in the Western United States and played a pioneering role in popularizing space science education and public outreach. Named in honor of Max C. Fleischmann, a prominent philanthropist and supporter of science education, the planetarium has been a beloved destination for visitors of all ages for over half a century.

- Immersive Experiences: Attend a live star show or planetarium presentation to learn about the night sky and celestial phenomena, or participate in hands-on science demonstrations and workshops led by knowledgeable educators. Explore the planetarium's exhibit hall, which features interactive displays, models, and artifacts related to astronomy, space exploration, and scientific discovery.

- Practical Information: The Fleischmann Planetarium and Science Center is located at 1650 N. Virginia St. on the campus of the University of Nevada, Reno. It is open Tuesday through Sunday, with extended hours on select days. Admission fees vary depending on age and residency, with discounts available for seniors, students, and military personnel. Parking is available at the planetarium, with additional parking available nearby. Be sure to check the planetarium's website for current hours of operation and show schedules.

10. Idlewild Park: Natural Wonder

- Description: Idlewild Park is a picturesque urban oasis located along the Truckee River in downtown Reno. Spanning over 49 acres, the park features lush green spaces, mature trees, and scenic waterways, making it a popular destination for outdoor recreation, picnicking, and family gatherings.

- Features: Visitors to Idlewild Park can enjoy a variety of amenities and activities, including playgrounds, sports fields, picnic areas, and walking paths. The park is home to a beautiful rose garden, a skate park, and an outdoor amphitheater that hosts concerts, festivals, and special events throughout the year.
- Historical Significance: Idlewild Park was established in the early 20th century as a public park and recreation area for the residents of Reno. Over the years, it has undergone numerous renovations and improvements, including the addition of new facilities and landscaping features that enhance its beauty and accessibility.
- Immersive Experiences: Take a leisurely stroll along the park's walking paths, which wind through shaded groves and scenic overlooks of the Truckee River. Rent a paddleboat or kayak and explore the river, or enjoy a game of frisbee golf or volleyball with friends and family.
- Practical Information: Idlewild Park is located at 2055 Idlewild Dr. in downtown Reno, adjacent to the Truckee River. It is open daily, with free admission and parking. Visitors can access the park via several entrances, including Idlewild Dr., Booth St., and Riverside Dr. Be sure to bring sunscreen, water, and snacks, as amenities such as restrooms and concessions may be limited.

11. Animal Ark Wildlife Sanctuary: Natural Wonder

- Description: Animal Ark Wildlife Sanctuary is a unique conservation facility located just north of Reno, dedicated to the rescue, rehabilitation, and conservation of North American wildlife. Situated on over 38 acres of natural habitat, the sanctuary provides a safe haven for orphaned, injured, and displaced animals, including wolves, bears, cougars, and raptors.

- Features: Visitors to Animal Ark can embark on guided walking tours of the sanctuary to observe and learn about its resident animals in their natural habitats. The sanctuary's knowledgeable staff and volunteers provide educational programs and presentations that highlight the importance of wildlife conservation and habitat preservation.

- Historical Significance: Animal Ark was founded in 1981 by Aaron and Diana Hiibel as a nonprofit organization dedicated to the welfare and conservation of wildlife. Over the years, the sanctuary has rescued and rehabilitated hundreds of animals, many of which cannot be released back into the wild due to injury or human imprinting.

- Immersive Experiences: Attend a special event or behind-the-scenes tour at Animal Ark, where you can meet and interact with sanctuary staff and learn about the daily care and feeding of the animals. Participate in volunteer opportunities and conservation projects, or support the sanctuary's mission through donations and sponsorship.

- Practical Information: Animal Ark Wildlife Sanctuary is located at 1265 Deerlodge Rd. in Reno, approximately a 30-minute drive from downtown. It is open seasonally from April to November, with limited hours and days of operation. Admission fees vary depending on age and residency, with discounts available for seniors, students, and military personnel. Parking is available at the sanctuary, with additional parking available nearby. Be sure to check the sanctuary's website for current hours of operation and tour availability.

12. Pioneer Center for the Performing Arts: Cultural Site

- Description: The Pioneer Center for the Performing Arts is a premier cultural venue located in downtown Reno, dedicated to presenting and promoting the performing arts in Northern Nevada. Housed in a distinctive architectural landmark known for its iconic copper-clad geodesic dome, the Pioneer Center hosts a diverse array of performances, including music, theater, dance, and comedy.

- Features: Visitors to the Pioneer Center can enjoy a wide range of performances and events throughout the year, including Broadway musicals, symphony concerts, ballet recitals, and comedy shows. The center's state-of-the-art facilities include a main stage theater with seating for over 1,500 guests, as well as smaller performance spaces and rehearsal studios.

- Historical Significance: The Pioneer Center for the Performing Arts was built in 1967 as part of the urban renewal efforts in downtown Reno, designed by renowned architect Frederic DeLongchamps. Over the years, it has become a cultural landmark and gathering place for the community, hosting world-class artists and productions from around the globe.

- Immersive Experiences: Attend a live performance or concert at the Pioneer Center to experience the magic of the performing arts up close. Take a backstage tour of the theater to learn about its history, architecture, and technical capabilities, or participate in educational programs and workshops offered by resident arts organizations.

- Practical Information: The Pioneer Center for the Performing Arts is located at 100 S. Virginia St. in downtown Reno, adjacent to the Truckee River. It is open year-round, with performances scheduled throughout the week. Ticket prices vary depending on the event and seating location, with discounts available for seniors, students, and members. Parking is available at nearby public parking garages and metered street parking. Be sure to check the center's website for current performance schedules and ticket availability.

13. Terry Lee Wells Nevada Discovery Museum: Cultural Site

- Description: The Terry Lee Wells Nevada Discovery Museum, also known as The Discovery, is a hands-on science museum located in downtown Reno, dedicated to inspiring curiosity, creativity, and lifelong learning through interactive exhibits and educational programs. Housed in a modern facility designed for exploration and discovery, The Discovery offers a wide range of exhibits and activities for visitors of all ages.
- Features: Visitors to The Discovery can explore a variety of galleries and play areas that cover topics such as physics, chemistry, biology, geology, and astronomy. The museum's exhibits encourage hands-on experimentation, critical thinking, and problem-solving skills, making learning fun and engaging for visitors of all ages.
- Historical Significance: The Terry Lee Wells Nevada Discovery Museum was founded in 2011 as a nonprofit organization dedicated to providing informal science education and enrichment opportunities for the community. Named in honor of philanthropist Terry Lee Wells, the

museum has quickly become a popular destination for families, schools, and visitors from near and far.

- Immersive Experiences: Participate in interactive science demonstrations and workshops led by museum educators, or attend special events and themed programs that explore scientific concepts and principles in depth. Explore the museum's outdoor science park, which features hands-on exhibits, a climbing wall, and a nature trail.

- Practical Information: The Terry Lee Wells Nevada Discovery Museum is located at 490 S. Center St. in downtown Reno, adjacent to the Truckee River. It is open Tuesday through Sunday, with extended hours on select days. Admission fees vary depending on age and residency, with discounts available for seniors, students, and military personnel. Parking is available at nearby public parking garages and metered street parking. Be sure to check the museum's website for current hours of operation and special exhibitions.

14. Riverwalk District: Cultural Site

- Description: The Riverwalk District in downtown Reno is a vibrant and scenic area that runs along the banks of the Truckee River. Known for its bustling atmosphere, the district is a hub of activity featuring a mix of restaurants, shops, galleries, and entertainment venues. The district's picturesque riverfront setting and lively events make it a popular destination for both locals and visitors.

- Features: The Riverwalk District offers a wide range of attractions and activities. Visitors can enjoy a leisurely stroll along the river, dine at a variety of restaurants offering everything from casual bites to fine dining, and explore unique boutiques and art galleries. The district is also home to several key landmarks and attractions, including the Reno Arch, Wingfield Park, and the Aces Ballpark.

- Historical Significance: The Riverwalk District has played a crucial role in Reno's development and revitalization efforts. Historically, the Truckee River was central to the city's growth, providing water for early settlers and serving as a hub for commerce and transportation. In recent decades, the area has been revitalized to become a cultural and recreational hotspot, blending historic charm with modern amenities.

- Immersive Experiences: Attend one of the many events held in the Riverwalk District, such as the monthly Wine Walk, which allows participants to sample wines from various local establishments, or the Riverwalk Merchants Association's Dine the District Food Tour, which showcases the culinary diversity of the area. Visitors can also enjoy outdoor concerts and festivals at Wingfield Park, which is located on an island in the river and accessible by pedestrian bridges.

- Practical Information: The Riverwalk District is located in the heart of downtown Reno, stretching along the Truckee River from Arlington Avenue to Lake Street. It is easily accessible by foot, bike, or public transportation. Parking is available in nearby garages and metered street parking. Many of the district's attractions and events are free to the public, although specific activities, such as the Wine Walk, may require a fee for participation. Check the Riverwalk District's website or visitor center for a current calendar of events and more detailed information on the area's offerings.

15. Reno Arch: Iconic Landmark

- Description: The Reno Arch is an iconic symbol of the city, welcoming visitors with its famous slogan, "The Biggest Little City in the World." Located in the heart of downtown Reno on Virginia Street, the arch is a beloved landmark and a popular photo spot for tourists.
- Features: The current Reno Arch, installed in 1987, is the third iteration of the landmark, featuring neon lights and a retro design that pays homage to the city's vibrant history. The arch is illuminated at night, creating a striking visual centerpiece for the downtown area. Surrounding the arch are numerous shops, restaurants, and casinos, making it a bustling and lively part of the city.
- Historical Significance: The original Reno Arch was erected in 1926 to commemorate the completion of the Lincoln and Victory Highways, the first transcontinental roads in the United States. Over the decades, the arch has been redesigned and relocated, but it has remained a constant symbol of Reno's welcoming spirit and its reputation as a major destination for entertainment and tourism.
- Immersive Experiences: Capture the perfect photo under the arch, especially at night when its lights create a dazzling display. Explore the surrounding downtown area, which is home to some of Reno's best dining, shopping, and entertainment options. Attend one of the many events and festivals that take place near the arch throughout the

year, such as the Reno River Festival or the Hot August Nights car show.

- Practical Information: The Reno Arch is located at 155 N. Virginia St. in downtown Reno, near the intersection with Commercial Row. It is easily accessible by foot, car, or public transportation. Parking is available in nearby public garages and metered street parking. There is no admission fee to visit the arch, and it is open to the public 24/7. Be sure to check the city's event calendar for information on upcoming festivals and activities in the area.

These must-visit attractions in Reno offer a diverse range of experiences, from exploring the city's rich history and culture to immersing oneself in the natural beauty of the surrounding landscape. Whether you're interested in outdoor adventures, cultural attractions, or educational experiences, Reno has something to offer every traveler. Be sure to plan your visit accordingly, taking into account factors such as location, hours of operation, and admission fees, to make the most of your time in this vibrant and dynamic destination.

Day Trips from Reno

Reno is not only a vibrant city with a wealth of attractions but also a fantastic base for exploring the surrounding region. From picturesque lakes to historic towns and stunning natural landscapes, there are numerous exciting day trips that cater to a variety of interests. Here are outstanding day trip options from Reno, each offering unique experiences and unforgettable adventures.

1. Lake Tahoe

Overview

- Just a short drive from Reno, Lake Tahoe is a must-visit destination for anyone exploring the area. Known for its crystal-clear waters and stunning mountain scenery, Lake Tahoe offers a wealth of activities year-round, from winter sports to summer water adventures.

Highlights

- Water Activities: In the summer, Lake Tahoe is a paradise for water enthusiasts. Enjoy swimming, kayaking, paddleboarding, or simply relaxing on one of the many beautiful beaches, such as Sand Harbor or Kings Beach.
- Hiking and Biking: The surrounding mountains provide ample opportunities for hiking and biking. Popular trails include the Tahoe Rim Trail and the Eagle Falls Trail, which offer breathtaking views of the lake and surrounding wilderness.
- Winter Sports: In the winter, Lake Tahoe transforms into a snowy wonderland. Renowned ski resorts like Squaw Valley and Heavenly offer world-class skiing, snowboarding, and other winter activities.
- Scenic Drives: The 72-mile drive around Lake Tahoe is one of the most scenic routes in the United States. It offers numerous spots to stop and take in the panoramic views, including Emerald Bay, a popular vista point known for its stunning beauty.

Travel Logistics

- Transportation: Lake Tahoe is approximately a one-hour drive from Reno. Renting a car is the most convenient way to explore the area, giving you flexibility to visit multiple spots around the lake.

- Entrance Fees: There are no general entrance fees for Lake Tahoe, but some specific attractions and parks may charge a fee. For example, Sand Harbor charges a small parking fee.
- Operating Hours: The lake and its surroundings are accessible year-round. However, specific attractions and facilities may have seasonal hours.
- Dining Recommendations: For a lakeside meal, visit Edgewood Restaurant in Stateline for upscale dining with spectacular views, or head to Fire Sign Café in Tahoe City for a cozy, casual breakfast or lunch.

2. Virginia City

Overview

- Step back in time with a visit to Virginia City, a historic mining town located about 25 miles southeast of Reno. Once a booming center during the Gold Rush era, Virginia City offers a fascinating glimpse into the past with its preserved buildings, museums, and charming streets.

Highlights

- Historic Downtown: Wander through the well-preserved downtown area, where you can explore old saloons, shops, and museums. The town's wooden boardwalks and vintage storefronts transport you to the 19th century.
- The Comstock Lode: Learn about the rich mining history of Virginia City at the Comstock Lode, one of the most significant silver deposits ever discovered. Visit the Virginia City Mining Company to see mining artifacts and exhibits.

- The Virginia & Truckee Railroad: Enjoy a scenic train ride on the historic Virginia & Truckee Railroad, which offers a journey through the picturesque high desert landscape. The train departs from the Virginia City depot and provides an authentic experience of 19th-century rail travel.
- The Washoe Club: For those intrigued by the paranormal, a visit to the Washoe Club is a must. This historic saloon and haunted museum is known for its ghostly legends and was even featured on the TV show "Ghost Adventures."

Travel Logistics

- Transportation: Virginia City is a short 40-minute drive from Reno. Driving is the most practical option, but you can also take a guided tour from Reno if you prefer.
- Entrance Fees: Walking around Virginia City is free, but certain attractions like museums and the train ride have admission fees.
- Operating Hours: Many of the town's attractions are open year-round, but check specific venues for their operating hours, especially in the winter months.
- Dining Recommendations: Enjoy a meal at the Café Del Rio, known for its delicious Southwestern cuisine, or step into the historic Bucket of Blood Saloon for a drink and a bite in a classic Old West setting.

3. Truckee

Overview

- Nestled in the Sierra Nevada mountains, the charming town of Truckee offers a mix of outdoor adventures, historical sites, and a vibrant arts scene. Located about 30 miles west of Reno, Truckee is an ideal destination for those looking to explore nature and history.

Highlights

- Historic Downtown Truckee: Stroll through Truckee's historic downtown, which is lined with quaint shops, art galleries, and restaurants. The town's well-preserved buildings and unique character make it a delightful place to explore.
- Donner Memorial State Park: Visit Donner Memorial State Park to learn about the famous Donner Party and their harrowing journey through the Sierra Nevada. The park features a museum, interpretive trails, and picnic areas.
- Outdoor Activities: Truckee is surrounded by natural beauty, offering numerous outdoor activities. In the summer, enjoy hiking, mountain biking, and fishing. In the winter, nearby ski resorts like Northstar and Sugar Bowl provide excellent skiing and snowboarding opportunities.
- Art and Culture: Truckee has a thriving arts community. Visit the Truckee Public Art Trail or the Truckee Cultural District to explore local art installations and cultural events.

Travel Logistics

- Transportation: Truckee is a 35-minute drive from Reno. Renting a car is recommended for flexibility, but there are also bus services available.
- Entrance Fees: Downtown Truckee and most outdoor activities are free, though some attractions like Donner Memorial State Park charge a small entrance fee.

- Operating Hours: Most attractions in Truckee are open year-round, but hours may vary seasonally. Check specific venues for details.
- Dining Recommendations: For a hearty meal, head to the Squeeze In for breakfast or lunch, famous for its omelets. For dinner, enjoy farm-to-table dining at the Truckee Tavern & Grill.

4. Pyramid Lake

Overview

- Pyramid Lake, located about 40 miles northeast of Reno, is a stunning desert lake known for its unique geology and cultural significance to the Paiute Tribe. The lake's turquoise waters and dramatic rock formations create a captivating landscape.

Highlights

- Fishing: Pyramid Lake is renowned for its Lahontan cutthroat trout, attracting anglers from around the world. The lake offers some of the best fishing in the region.
- Outdoor Recreation: Beyond fishing, the lake is ideal for boating, kayaking, and swimming. The expansive shoreline provides plenty of space for relaxation and picnicking.
- Cultural Significance: Explore the cultural history of the Paiute Tribe, who have inhabited the area for thousands of years. Visit the Pyramid Lake Museum and Visitors Center in Nixon to learn about the tribe's heritage and the lake's ecological significance.
- Scenic Beauty: The lake's namesake, the Pyramid, is a striking tufa formation that rises from the water. Other

notable formations include the Stone Mother and Anaho Island, home to a large American white pelican nesting colony.

Travel Logistics

- Transportation: Pyramid Lake is approximately a 50-minute drive from Reno. Renting a car is the most convenient way to reach the lake and explore its surroundings.
- Entrance Fees: A tribal permit is required to access the lake for fishing and other recreational activities. Permits can be purchased online or at local vendors.
- Operating Hours: The lake and its attractions are accessible year-round, but the best time to visit is during the spring and fall when the weather is most pleasant.
- Dining Recommendations: There are limited dining options near the lake, so it's a good idea to bring a picnic. Alternatively, visit the nearby town of Nixon for basic amenities and local eateries.

Practical Tips for Day Trips from Reno

Transportation Options

- Car Rentals: Renting a car is highly recommended for flexibility and convenience. Major rental companies operate in Reno, and it's easy to book a vehicle in advance.
- Public Transit: Some day trip destinations are accessible via public transit, such as buses or trains, but schedules and routes may be limited.

- Guided Tours: Consider booking a guided tour for a hassle-free experience. Many local tour operators offer day trips to popular destinations with transportation included.

What to Bring

- Essentials: Pack essentials such as water, snacks, sunscreen, and comfortable walking shoes. A hat and sunglasses are also recommended for sun protection.
- Layers: Weather can vary, especially in mountainous areas, so bring layers to stay comfortable.
- Camera: Don't forget your camera to capture the stunning landscapes and memorable moments.

Planning Your Itinerary

- Start Early: Begin your day trip early to make the most of your time and avoid crowds at popular attractions.
- Check Hours: Verify the operating hours and any seasonal closures of attractions before you go.
- Reservations: For dining or guided tours, make reservations in advance to secure your spot.

Safety Tips

- Stay Hydrated: Drink plenty of water, especially if you're spending time outdoors.
- Know Your Limits: Choose activities that match your fitness level and experience. Be mindful of altitude and weather conditions.
- Respect Local Regulations: Follow local rules and guidelines, particularly in protected natural areas and cultural sites.

Reno's prime location makes it an ideal starting point for a variety of captivating day trips. Whether you're drawn to the sparkling waters of Lake Tahoe, the historic charm of Virginia City, the outdoor adventures in Truckee, or the serene beauty of Pyramid Lake, each destination offers unique experiences that will enrich your visit. With practical tips and detailed information at your fingertips, you're well-equipped to embark on these memorable journeys and explore the diverse landscapes and attractions just a short distance from Reno.

CHAPTER 6

OUTDOOR ACTIVITIES AND ADVENTURES

Reno, nestled in the foothills of the Sierra Nevada Mountains, offers an abundance of outdoor activities and adventures for nature lovers and thrill-seekers alike. With its stunning landscapes, diverse ecosystems, and favorable climate, the region provides a perfect playground for outdoor enthusiasts. Whether you're looking for adrenaline-pumping adventure sports or serene nature walks, Reno has something for everyone. Here, we explore and highlight the diverse range of outdoor experiences available, providing comprehensive information to help you plan your outdoor adventures.

Hiking Trails

Reno and its surrounding areas are a paradise for hiking enthusiasts, offering a diverse range of trails that wind through picturesque landscapes, from rugged desert canyons to alpine forests. Whether you're seeking a leisurely stroll or a challenging trek, there's a hiking trail to suit every preference and skill level. Lace up your hiking boots and explore the natural beauty of the Reno-Tahoe region on these top hiking trails.

1. Hunter Creek Trail

Overview

- Located just minutes from downtown Reno, the Hunter Creek Trail is a popular hiking destination that offers stunning views of the Sierra Nevada Mountains and the

Truckee Meadows below. The trail meanders along Hunter Creek, passing through shady forests, rocky outcrops, and scenic meadows.

Trail Features

- Distance: Approximately 6 miles round trip
- Difficulty: Moderate
- Elevation Gain: 900 feet
- Trailhead: Located off Woodchuck Circle in Reno

Highlights

- Waterfall: The highlight of the hike is the picturesque Hunter Creek waterfall, which cascades over a series of rocky ledges and pools.
- Scenic Views: Along the trail, hikers are treated to panoramic views of the surrounding mountains and valleys, including Mt. Rose and the Virginia Range.
- Wildlife: Keep an eye out for wildlife, including deer, rabbits, and a variety of bird species that inhabit the area.

Tips

- Bring Water: Be sure to bring plenty of water, especially on hot days, as there are limited opportunities to refill along the trail.
- Wear Sunscreen: Parts of the trail are exposed to the sun, so wear sunscreen and a hat to protect against sunburn.
- Pack Out Trash: Practice Leave No Trace principles and pack out any trash or waste to help preserve the natural beauty of the area.

2. Tahoe Rim Trail: Mount Rose Summit

Overview

- The Tahoe Rim Trail is a 165-mile loop that circumnavigates the Lake Tahoe Basin, offering some of the most scenic hiking in the region. The section leading to Mount Rose Summit provides breathtaking views of Lake Tahoe, the Carson Valley, and the surrounding mountains.

Trail Features

- Distance: Approximately 10 miles round trip
- Difficulty: Strenuous
- Elevation Gain: 2,300 feet
- Trailhead: Mount Rose Summit Trailhead off Highway 431

Highlights

- Summit Views: The trail climbs steadily to the summit of Mount Rose, the highest peak in the Carson Range, where hikers are rewarded with sweeping views in all directions.
- Alpine Meadows: Along the way, hikers pass through lush alpine meadows dotted with wildflowers during the summer months.
- Wildlife Viewing: Keep an eye out for mule deer, chipmunks, and other wildlife that inhabit the area.

Tips

- Start Early: Begin your hike early in the day to avoid afternoon thunderstorms and to enjoy cooler temperatures at higher elevations.
- Be Prepared: Bring plenty of water, snacks, and layers of clothing, as weather conditions can change rapidly in the mountains.

- Stay on Trail: Stick to designated trails to protect fragile alpine ecosystems and minimize erosion.

3. Galena Creek Trail

Overview

- Located in Galena Creek Regional Park, the Galena Creek Trail offers a scenic and family-friendly hike through pine forests, meadows, and along the banks of Galena Creek. The trail provides a peaceful escape from the hustle and bustle of city life.

Trail Features

- Distance: Approximately 4 miles round trip
- Difficulty: Easy to moderate
- Elevation Gain: Minimal
- Trailhead: Galena Creek Visitor Center off Mount Rose Highway

Highlights

- Creek Crossing: The trail crosses Galena Creek via a wooden footbridge, offering opportunities to cool off and enjoy the sounds of running water.
- Wildflowers: During the spring and summer months, the trail is lined with colorful wildflowers, including lupine, Indian paintbrush, and columbine.
- Interpretive Signs: Along the trail, hikers can learn about the area's natural history and ecology through interpretive signs and displays.

Tips

- Check Trail Conditions: Some sections of the trail may be muddy or icy, especially during the winter and spring months, so wear appropriate footwear and use caution.
- Bring Binoculars: The trail is home to a variety of bird species, so bring binoculars for birdwatching opportunities.
- Explore Further: The Galena Creek Nature Trail and Jones Creek Loop Trail branch off from the main trail, offering additional hiking options for those looking to extend their adventure.

4. Mount Rose Trail

Overview

- The Mount Rose Trail is a challenging but rewarding hike that leads to the summit of Mount Rose, the highest peak in the Lake Tahoe Basin. The trail offers panoramic views of Lake Tahoe, the Sierra Nevada Mountains, and the surrounding valleys.

Trail Features

- Distance: Approximately 10 miles round trip
- Difficulty: Strenuous
- Elevation Gain: 2,300 feet
- Trailhead: Mount Rose Summit Trailhead off Highway 431

Highlights

- Summit Views: The trail climbs steadily through forests and meadows to the summit of Mount Rose, where hikers are treated to breathtaking views of Lake Tahoe and the surrounding mountains.

- Alpine Lakes: Along the way, hikers pass by picturesque alpine lakes, including Mount Rose Lake and Tahoe Meadows.
- Fall Colors: During the autumn months, the trail is ablaze with vibrant fall foliage, making it an especially scenic hike.

Tips

- Start Early: Begin your hike early in the day to avoid afternoon thunderstorms and to enjoy cooler temperatures at higher elevations.
- Stay Hydrated: Bring plenty of water, as there are limited water sources along the trail.
- Be Prepared: Dress in layers and be prepared for changing weather conditions, especially at higher elevations.

Practical Tips for Hiking in Reno

- Check Trail Conditions: Before heading out, check trail conditions, weather forecasts, and any trail closures or restrictions.
- Bring Essentials: Carry essential items such as water, snacks, a map or GPS device, a first aid kit, and a flashlight or headlamp.
- Leave No Trace: Practice Leave No Trace principles and minimize your impact on the environment by staying on designated trails, packing out trash, and respecting wildlife.
- Tell Someone Your Plans: Always let someone know your hiking plans, including your intended route, expected return time, and emergency contact information.

- Be Prepared: Be prepared for changing weather conditions, wildlife encounters, and emergencies by carrying appropriate gear and knowing basic survival skills.

Whether you're seeking scenic vistas, serene forests, or challenging terrain, Reno's hiking trails offer something for everyone. Lace up your boots, hit the trail, and immerse yourself in the natural beauty of the Reno-Tahoe region.

Water Activities

Reno may be known for its desert landscapes, but it's also surrounded by waterways that offer a variety of recreational opportunities for water enthusiasts. From kayaking and paddleboarding to fishing and boating, there's no shortage of ways to enjoy the water in and around Reno. Dive in and explore the aquatic adventures waiting to be discovered.

1. Kayaking and Stand-Up Paddleboarding (SUP)

Overview

- Kayaking and stand-up paddleboarding (SUP) are popular water sports in Reno, offering a fun and scenic way to explore the region's rivers, lakes, and reservoirs. Whether you're gliding along the tranquil waters of Lake Tahoe or navigating the rapids of the Truckee River, kayaking and SUP provide a unique perspective of the area's natural beauty.

Popular Kayaking and SUP Locations

- Lake Tahoe: With its crystal-clear waters and stunning mountain backdrop, Lake Tahoe is a premier destination for kayaking and SUP. Rent a kayak or paddleboard from one of the many outfitters along the shore and explore the lake's pristine bays and coves.

- Truckee River: The Truckee River runs right through downtown Reno, offering a convenient and scenic paddling experience. Rent a kayak or SUP from one of the local outfitters and paddle through the heart of the city, taking in views of the surrounding skyline and natural scenery.
- Donner Lake: Located just west of Truckee, Donner Lake is a picturesque alpine lake surrounded by towering peaks. Rent a kayak or SUP and explore the calm waters of the lake, or venture out to the nearby Donner Memorial State Park for additional paddling opportunities.

Equipment Rentals and Guided Tours

- Local outfitters and rental shops offer a variety of kayaks, paddleboards, and equipment for rent, as well as guided tours and lessons for beginners. Guided tours provide instruction, safety tips, and insights into the area's natural and cultural history, making them ideal for first-time paddlers.

Safety Considerations

- Wear a PFD: Always wear a personal flotation device (PFD) while kayaking or SUP, and ensure it fits properly and securely.
- Know Your Limits: Choose paddling locations and routes that match your skill level and experience, and avoid areas with strong currents or hazards.

- Check Weather Conditions: Keep an eye on weather forecasts and avoid paddling in inclement weather or high winds.
- Stay Hydrated: Bring plenty of water and stay hydrated, especially on hot days when paddling can be physically demanding.

Best Times for Kayaking and SUP

- Kayaking and SUP can be enjoyed year-round in Reno, although water temperatures and weather conditions vary by season. Summer and early fall are the most popular times for paddling, with warmer temperatures and calmer waters, while spring offers opportunities for paddling as snowmelt increases water levels in rivers and lakes.

2. Fishing

Overview

- Fishing is a beloved pastime in Reno, with a variety of lakes, rivers, and streams teeming with trout, bass, and other freshwater species. Whether you're fly fishing in a mountain stream or casting a line from the shores of a tranquil lake, Reno offers abundant opportunities for anglers of all skill levels.

Popular Fishing Locations

- Truckee River: The Truckee River is a popular fishing destination that runs through downtown Reno and offers excellent trout fishing opportunities. Anglers can target rainbow, brown, and cutthroat trout in the river's clear, cold waters.

- Pyramid Lake: Located northeast of Reno on the Pyramid Lake Paiute Tribe Reservation, Pyramid Lake is renowned for its world-class Lahontan cutthroat trout fishing. The lake's unique ecosystem and scenic beauty make it a favorite among anglers seeking trophy-sized fish.
- Donner Lake: Donner Lake is a picturesque alpine lake known for its abundance of rainbow and brown trout. Anglers can fish from the shore, a boat, or a kayak, and enjoy stunning views of the surrounding Sierra Nevada Mountains.

Fishing Regulations

- Before heading out, be sure to familiarize yourself with local fishing regulations, including license requirements, catch limits, and seasonal closures. Some fishing areas may have specific rules and regulations in place to protect sensitive habitats and fish populations, so check with local authorities or fishing guides for up-to-date information.

Equipment and Gear

- Anglers can purchase fishing licenses, tackle, bait, and other equipment from local bait shops, outdoor outfitters, or sporting goods stores. Fly fishing enthusiasts will find a variety of fly shops and guides offering gear rentals, lessons, and guided trips on the area's rivers and streams.

Best Times for Fishing

- Fishing season in Reno varies depending on the species and location, but generally runs from spring through fall, with peak fishing times occurring in the early morning and late afternoon. Spring and fall offer excellent trout fishing opportunities, while summer provides warmer water temperatures and the chance to catch bass and other warmwater species.

3. Boating

Overview

- Boating is a popular recreational activity in Reno, with a variety of lakes and reservoirs offering opportunities for sailing, motorboating, and waterskiing. Whether you're cruising along the shores of Lake Tahoe or exploring the hidden coves of Donner Lake, boating provides a fun and scenic way to enjoy the water.

Popular Boating Locations

- Lake Tahoe: With its crystal-clear waters and stunning mountain backdrop, Lake Tahoe is a premier boating destination. Boaters can enjoy sailing, powerboating, kayaking, and paddleboarding on the lake, as well as exploring its numerous beaches and bays.
- Donner Lake: Donner Lake is a picturesque alpine lake located just west of Truckee, offering calm waters and scenic surroundings for boating enthusiasts. Visitors can rent pontoon boats, kayaks, or paddleboards from local outfitters and explore the lake's tranquil coves and inlets.
- Pyramid Lake: Pyramid Lake is a unique and scenic destination for boating, with its striking blue waters and iconic rock formations. Boaters can launch from designated areas along the shoreline and explore the lake's vast expanse, fishing for Lahontan cutthroat trout or simply enjoying the serene beauty of the landscape.

Boat Rentals and Marinas

- Local marinas and boat rental shops offer a variety of watercraft for rent, including motorboats, sailboats, kayaks, and paddleboards. Whether you're looking for a leisurely cruise or an adrenaline-pumping waterskiing adventure, there's a boat rental option to suit every preference and budget.

Safety Considerations

- Life Jackets: Ensure that all passengers have access to properly fitting life jackets and wear them at all times while on the water.
- Boating Rules: Familiarize yourself with local boating regulations and rules of the waterway, including speed limits, navigation rules, and no-wake zones.
- Weather Awareness: Keep an eye on weather forecasts and be prepared to return to shore if conditions deteriorate or if thunderstorms are approaching.
- Boat Maintenance: Perform regular maintenance checks on your boat, including inspecting the engine, checking fuel levels, and ensuring that safety equipment is in good working order.

Best Times for Boating

- Boating season in Reno typically runs from late spring through early fall, with the warmest and most favorable weather conditions occurring during the summer months. Weekends and holidays tend to be the busiest times on the water, so plan accordingly and arrive early to secure parking and avoid crowds.

4. Whitewater Rafting

Overview

- For thrill-seekers and adrenaline junkies, whitewater rafting offers an exhilarating way to experience Reno's rivers and canyons. From gentle Class I rapids to heart-pounding Class V drops, there are whitewater rafting adventures for all skill levels and preferences.

Popular Whitewater Rafting Rivers

- Truckee River: The Truckee River offers a variety of whitewater rafting experiences, with sections ranging from calm stretches suitable for beginners to challenging rapids for experienced paddlers. Guided rafting trips are available on the Truckee River, providing a safe and exciting way to navigate the rapids.
- American River: Located a short drive from Reno, the American River is renowned for its thrilling whitewater rapids and scenic beauty. The South Fork of the American River is a popular rafting destination, offering Class III rapids and stunning canyon scenery.
- Carson River: The Carson River offers a more laid-back rafting experience, with gentle currents and scenic views of the surrounding mountains and valleys. Guided rafting trips are available on the Carson River, providing a fun and family-friendly way to explore the waterway.

Guided Tours and Safety

- For those new to whitewater rafting, guided tours are a great option, as experienced guides provide instruction, safety briefings, and equipment, ensuring a safe and enjoyable experience on the water. Guides are trained in swiftwater rescue techniques and are familiar with local river conditions, ensuring a memorable and hassle-free rafting adventure.

Equipment and Gear

- Whitewater rafting outfitters provide all necessary equipment, including rafts, paddles, helmets, and personal flotation devices (PFDs). Participants should wear appropriate clothing and footwear for the river conditions, including quick-drying clothing, water shoes, and sunscreen.

Best Times for Whitewater Rafting

- Whitewater rafting season in Reno typically runs from spring through early summer, when snowmelt from the surrounding mountains increases water levels and creates optimal conditions for rafting. Depending on river conditions and water levels, rafting may be available into the early fall months.

Practical Tips for Water Activities

- Book in Advance: Reserve rentals, guided tours, or lessons in advance, especially during peak season, to ensure availability.
- Know Your Limits: Choose activities and waterways that match your skill level and experience, and be honest about your abilities when assessing the difficulty of a particular activity.
- Stay Hydrated: Drink plenty of water to stay hydrated, especially during hot weather or strenuous activities.

- Be Respectful: Respect wildlife, other water users, and the natural environment by following Leave No Trace principles and minimizing your impact on the waterway.

From tranquil paddling excursions to adrenaline-pumping whitewater adventures, Reno's waterways offer endless opportunities for outdoor fun and exploration. Whether you're seeking a leisurely day on the lake or an adrenaline-pumping rafting trip, there's a water activity to suit every interest and skill level. Dive in and make a splash in Reno's aquatic playground!

Adventure Sports

Reno isn't just about casinos and nightlife; it's also a hub for adrenaline-pumping adventure sports that cater to thrill-seekers and outdoor enthusiasts. From rock climbing and mountain biking to whitewater rafting and skydiving, there's no shortage of heart-pounding activities to get your blood pumping. Dive into the exhilarating world of adventure sports in Reno, where the rugged terrain and scenic landscapes provide the perfect backdrop for unforgettable outdoor experiences.

1. Rock Climbing

Overview

- Reno and its surrounding areas boast an abundance of rock climbing opportunities for climbers of all skill levels. With towering cliffs, rugged canyons, and diverse rock formations, the region offers challenges for both beginners and experienced climbers.

Popular Climbing Areas

- Lovers Leap: Located near Lake Tahoe, Lovers Leap is a premier destination for traditional rock climbing. Its granite cliffs offer a variety of routes, from moderate multi-pitch climbs to challenging cracks and face climbs.
- Donner Summit: Situated just west of Truckee, Donner Summit is renowned for its steep granite walls and classic climbing routes. With over 400 routes ranging from easy to extremely difficult, it's a favorite among climbers seeking adventure.
- The Gorge: Located south of Reno near Carson City, The Gorge features limestone cliffs and sport climbing routes with breathtaking views of the Carson Valley. Its sunny aspect makes it an ideal winter climbing destination.

Difficulty Levels

- Beginner: Lovers Leap, The Gorge
- Intermediate: Donner Summit, The Gorge
- Advanced: Donner Summit, Lovers Leap

Equipment Rentals and Guided Tours

- Local outdoor outfitters and climbing gyms offer equipment rentals, guided climbs, and instructional courses for climbers of all levels. Guided tours are available for individuals and groups looking to explore the area's best climbing routes with experienced guides.

Safety Considerations

- Use Proper Gear: Wear a helmet and use appropriate climbing equipment, including ropes, harnesses, and protective gear.

- Check Conditions: Assess rock quality, weather conditions, and route difficulty before attempting a climb.
- Know Your Limits: Climb within your ability level and communicate with your climbing partners about your objectives and expectations.
- Practice Leave No Trace: Respect the environment and minimize your impact by following Leave No Trace principles and staying on designated trails.

Best Times for Rock Climbing

- Rock climbing can be enjoyed year-round in Reno, although conditions vary depending on the season. Spring and fall are typically the best times for climbing, with mild temperatures and stable weather conditions. Summer can be hot, while winter offers cooler temperatures but limited climbing options due to snow and ice.

2. Mountain Biking

Overview

- Reno's diverse terrain and extensive trail networks make it a paradise for mountain biking enthusiasts. From rugged singletrack trails to scenic alpine routes, there are endless opportunities to explore the region on two wheels.

Popular Mountain Biking Trails

- Peavine Mountain: Located on the northwest edge of Reno, Peavine Mountain offers a vast network of trails with stunning views of the city and surrounding mountains. Trails range from smooth, flowy singletrack to technical descents and rocky terrain.

- Tahoe Rim Trail: Stretching for 165 miles along the ridgeline of the Sierra Nevada, the Tahoe Rim Trail offers some of the most scenic mountain biking in the region. Sections near Reno provide challenging climbs, thrilling descents, and panoramic views of Lake Tahoe.
- Galena Creek Trail: Situated in Galena Creek Regional Park, this intermediate-level trail offers a picturesque ride through pine forests and meadows. With relatively gentle grades and well-maintained trails, it's perfect for riders of all abilities.

Difficulty Levels

- Easy: Galena Creek Trail
- Moderate: Peavine Mountain, Tahoe Rim Trail
- Advanced: Peavine Mountain, Tahoe Rim Trail

Equipment Rentals and Guided Tours

- Local bike shops and outdoor outfitters offer mountain bike rentals, trail maps, and guided tours for riders of all levels. Guided tours provide insights into the area's top trails and terrain, along with instruction and support from experienced guides.

Safety Considerations

- Wear Protective Gear: Always wear a helmet and appropriate protective gear while mountain biking.
- Know the Trails: Familiarize yourself with trail difficulty ratings, terrain features, and potential hazards before riding.
- Ride Responsibly: Respect other trail users, yield to uphill riders, and obey all trail signs and regulations.

- Carry Essentials: Bring plenty of water, snacks, a map or GPS device, and a first aid kit in case of emergencies.

Best Times for Mountain Biking

- Mountain biking season in Reno typically runs from late spring to early fall, with the best riding conditions occurring in the summer months. Trails at higher elevations may remain snow-covered until late spring or early summer, so check trail conditions and weather forecasts before heading out.

3. Skydiving

Overview

- For the ultimate adrenaline rush, skydiving offers an unparalleled experience of freefalling through the sky with breathtaking views of the Reno-Tahoe region. Whether you're a first-time jumper or an experienced skydiver, Reno's skydiving centers cater to all levels of thrill-seekers.

Popular Skydiving Centers

- Skydive Lake Tahoe: Located near Minden-Tahoe Airport, Skydive Lake Tahoe offers tandem skydiving experiences with stunning views of Lake Tahoe and the Sierra Nevada Mountains. First-time jumpers can experience the thrill of freefalling while securely attached to an experienced instructor.
- Skydive Truckee Tahoe: Situated in Truckee, Skydive Truckee Tahoe provides tandem skydiving adventures over the picturesque landscapes of the Truckee-Tahoe region. Jumpers can enjoy panoramic views of Lake Tahoe,

Donner Lake, and the surrounding mountains during their freefall experience.

Difficulty Levels

- Beginner: Tandem skydiving
- Intermediate: Accelerated Freefall (AFF) training
- Advanced: Experienced skydivers

Equipment and Training

- Skydiving centers provide all necessary equipment, including jumpsuits, helmets, goggles, and parachutes. Tandem skydiving requires minimal training, as jumpers are attached to an experienced instructor who handles the parachute deployment and landing. For those interested in becoming certified skydivers, accelerated freefall (AFF) training courses are available, which involve comprehensive instruction and supervised jumps.

Safety Considerations

- Follow Instructor's Guidance: Listen to your instructor and follow their instructions for exiting the aircraft, freefalling, and landing.
- Trust Your Gear: Skydiving equipment undergoes rigorous safety checks and maintenance to ensure reliability and performance.
- Know Emergency Procedures: Familiarize yourself with emergency procedures and protocols for parachute malfunctions or other safety concerns.
- Stay Calm and Enjoy: Embrace the thrill of freefalling and enjoy the exhilarating experience of skydiving.

Best Times for Skydiving

- Skydiving can be enjoyed year-round in Reno, weather permitting. Clear skies and calm winds are ideal conditions for skydiving, so check the weather forecast and skydiving center's operating hours before booking your jump.

Practical Tips for Adventure Sports in Reno

- Plan Ahead: Research your chosen activity and location, and make reservations for equipment rentals, guided tours, or lessons in advance.
- Dress Appropriately: Wear appropriate clothing and gear for your chosen activity and the weather conditions.
- Stay Hydrated: Drink plenty of water to stay hydrated, especially during outdoor activities.
- Listen to Your Body: Know your limits and take breaks as needed to rest and recharge.
- Respect Nature: Follow Leave No Trace principles and leave the environment as you found it, preserving natural habitats for future generations.

Reno's diverse landscape and abundance of outdoor recreation opportunities make it an ideal destination for adventure sports enthusiasts. Whether you're seeking the thrill of rock climbing, the exhilaration of mountain biking, or the adrenaline of skydiving, Reno has something for everyone. With careful planning, preparation, and a spirit of adventure, you can embark on unforgettable outdoor experiences that will leave you craving more.

Winter Sports

Reno and its surrounding areas transform into a winter wonderland during the colder months, offering a plethora of winter sports and activities for enthusiasts of all ages and skill levels. From skiing and snowboarding to snowshoeing and ice skating, there are numerous opportunities to embrace the winter season and enjoy the pristine landscapes blanketed in snow. Here, we delve into the exciting world of winter sports in Reno, providing comprehensive information to help you plan your snowy adventures.

1. Skiing and Snowboarding

Overview

- Reno serves as an ideal gateway to some of the best ski resorts in the Sierra Nevada Mountains. With world-class slopes, varied terrain, and abundant snowfall, skiing and snowboarding enthusiasts flock to the area to experience the thrill of carving through fresh powder.

Popular Ski Resorts

- Mt. Rose Ski Tahoe: Located just 25 minutes from downtown Reno, Mt. Rose Ski Tahoe offers spectacular views of Lake Tahoe and the surrounding mountains. With over 1,200 acres of terrain and an average annual snowfall of 350 inches, it caters to skiers and snowboarders of all levels.
- Heavenly Mountain Resort: Situated on the south shore of Lake Tahoe, Heavenly boasts the largest ski area in California and Nevada, with over 4,800 acres of terrain. Its wide-open groomed runs, challenging steeps, and breathtaking views attract visitors from around the world.

- Northstar California Resort: Northstar is renowned for its family-friendly atmosphere and upscale amenities. With meticulously groomed trails, terrain parks, and a charming alpine village, it offers a memorable winter experience for skiers and snowboarders of all abilities.
- Squaw Valley Alpine Meadows: Host of the 1960 Winter Olympics, Squaw Valley Alpine Meadows is a legendary destination for winter sports enthusiasts. Its vast and diverse terrain, including steep chutes, groomed runs, and terrain parks, provides endless opportunities for exploration and adventure.

Difficulty Levels

- Beginner: Mt. Rose Ski Tahoe, Northstar California Resort
- Intermediate: Squaw Valley Alpine Meadows, Northstar California Resort
- Advanced: Heavenly Mountain Resort, Squaw Valley Alpine Meadows

Equipment Rentals and Lessons

- All ski resorts offer equipment rentals and lessons for beginners and those looking to improve their skills. Rentals typically include skis, boots, poles, and helmets, while lessons are available for individuals and groups of all ages and abilities.

Safety Considerations

- Wear Protective Gear: Always wear a helmet and appropriate protective gear while skiing or snowboarding.
- Know Your Limits: Stay within your skill level and avoid venturing into terrain that exceeds your abilities.

- Observe Trail Signs: Pay attention to trail signs and warnings, and ski or snowboard in control at all times.
- Stay Hydrated and Warm: Drink plenty of water and dress in layers to stay comfortable in varying weather conditions.

Best Times for Skiing and Snowboarding

- The ski season in Reno typically runs from late November to early April, with peak conditions usually occurring between December and February. Weekdays generally offer smaller crowds and shorter lift lines compared to weekends and holidays.

2. Snowshoeing

Overview

Snowshoeing is a popular winter activity that allows outdoor enthusiasts to explore the serene winter landscapes at a slower pace. Reno and its surrounding areas boast a variety of snowshoeing trails, ranging from easy strolls to challenging treks through pristine wilderness.

Popular Snowshoeing Trails

- Galena Creek Park: Located just a short drive from Reno, Galena Creek Park offers several snowshoeing trails suitable for all skill levels. The Jones Creek Loop Trail and the Bitterbrush Trail provide scenic views of the surrounding mountains and forests.

- Tahoe Meadows: Situated on the shores of Lake Tahoe, Tahoe Meadows features a network of snowshoeing trails that meander through open meadows and pine forests. The

Tahoe Meadows Interpretive Trail is a family-friendly option with informational signs along the route.

- Donner Memorial State Park: Located near Truckee, Donner Memorial State Park offers snowshoeing trails with historical significance. The Emigrant Trail follows the route taken by early pioneers, while the Coldstream Valley Loop provides panoramic views of Donner Lake and the surrounding mountains.

Difficulty Levels

- Easy: Galena Creek Park, Tahoe Meadows
- Moderate: Tahoe Meadows, Donner Memorial State Park
- Challenging: Donner Memorial State Park

Equipment Rentals and Guided Tours

- Local outdoor outfitters and ski resorts offer snowshoe rentals and guided tours for individuals and groups. Guided tours often include equipment, instruction, and insights into the area's natural history and wildlife.

Safety Considerations

- Stay on Marked Trails: Stick to designated snowshoeing trails and avoid venturing off-trail, especially in areas with avalanche danger.
- Be Prepared: Carry essential gear, including water, snacks, a map or GPS device, and extra clothing layers.
- Check Avalanche Conditions: Before heading out, check avalanche forecasts and avoid areas with high avalanche risk.

- Notify Someone of Your Plans: Inform a friend or family member of your itinerary and expected return time, especially if venturing into remote areas.

Best Times for Snowshoeing

- Snowshoeing can be enjoyed throughout the winter season, depending on snow conditions. Trails are typically well-groomed and accessible from late November to early April, with peak conditions occurring after fresh snowfall.

3. Ice Skating

Overview

- Ice skating is a classic winter pastime that offers fun for the whole family. Reno features several outdoor and indoor ice skating rinks where visitors can glide across the ice and enjoy the festive atmosphere.

Popular Ice Skating Rinks

- Reno Ice Rink: Located at Greater Nevada Field in downtown Reno, the Reno Ice Rink is a popular spot for ice skating enthusiasts. The outdoor rink offers public skating sessions, skate rentals, and special events throughout the winter season.
- Heavenly Village Ice Rink: Situated in the heart of Heavenly Village at South Lake Tahoe, this outdoor ice skating rink offers picturesque views of the surrounding mountains. Visitors can skate under the twinkling lights of the village and enjoy music and entertainment.
- Squaw Valley Ice Pavilion: The Olympic-sized ice skating rink at Squaw Valley Alpine Meadows provides a unique skating experience against the backdrop of the Sierra

Nevada Mountains. The rink offers public skating sessions, figure skating lessons, and hockey programs.

Equipment Rentals and Lessons

- Ice skating rinks typically offer skate rentals for visitors who don't have their own equipment. Many rinks also provide lessons for beginners, including group lessons and private instruction.

Safety Considerations

- Wear Warm Clothing: Dress in layers to stay warm while skating, and wear gloves or mittens to protect your hands.
- Skate Safely: Follow the rules and guidelines of the skating rink, and skate in the same direction as other skaters.
- Use Caution: Be mindful of ice conditions and potential hazards on the ice, such as cracks or rough patches.
- Supervise Children: Keep an eye on children while they skate, and ensure they stay within designated areas.

Best Times for Ice Skating

- Outdoor ice skating rinks typically operate from late November to early April, weather permitting. Weekends and holidays tend to be the busiest times, so visiting on weekdays or during off-peak hours can provide a more relaxed skating experience.

4. Snow Tubing

Overview

- Snow tubing offers an exhilarating and family-friendly way to experience the thrill of sledding without the hassle of climbing back up the hill. Reno and its surrounding areas feature snow tubing parks where visitors can slide down groomed lanes and enjoy the winter fun.

Popular Snow Tubing Parks

- Tahoe Donner Snowplay: Located in Truckee, Tahoe Donner Snowplay offers snow tubing fun for all ages. The park features multiple tubing lanes with varying degrees of steepness, as well as a warming hut and snack bar.
- Heavenly Mountain Resort Tubing Hill: Heavenly Mountain Resort's tubing hill offers panoramic views of Lake Tahoe and the surrounding mountains. The park provides tubing lanes, magic carpets for easy access to the top of the hill, and a lodge with hot cocoa and snacks.
- Squaw Valley SnoVentures Activity Zone: Squaw Valley Alpine Meadows' SnoVentures Activity Zone features a tubing hill, mini snowmobiles, and other winter activities. The tubing hill offers multiple lanes for tubing fun, with convenient access to the lodge and other amenities.

Equipment Rentals and Sessions

- Snow tubing parks typically provide tubes for visitors to use, along with access to the tubing lanes for a set duration of time. Sessions may be sold in blocks of time, such as one or two hours, and may include unlimited tubing during the session.

Safety Considerations

- Follow Instructions: Listen to the staff's instructions and guidelines for safe tubing, including how to enter and exit the tubing lanes.

- Be Aware of Surroundings: Pay attention to other tubers and your surroundings while tubing, and avoid collisions with other tubers or obstacles.
- Use Caution: Tubing hills may have varying degrees of steepness and speeds, so use caution and adjust your speed as needed.
- Supervise Children: Keep an eye on children while they tube and ensure they follow safety rules and guidelines.

Best Times for Snow Tubing

- Snow tubing parks typically operate from late November to early April, weather permitting. Weekends and holidays tend to be the busiest times, so visiting on weekdays or during off-peak hours can provide shorter wait times and more tubing fun.

Practical Tips for Winter Sports in Reno

- Check Conditions: Before heading out, check weather forecasts, snow conditions, and trail or rink statuses.
- Dress Appropriately: Layer clothing to stay warm and dry, and wear waterproof or insulated gear as needed.
- Stay Hydrated: Drink plenty of water to stay hydrated, even in cold weather.
- Know Your Limits: Choose activities and trails that match your skill level and experience, and avoid pushing yourself beyond your abilities.
- Plan Ahead: Make reservations for equipment rentals, lessons, or guided tours in advance, especially during peak times.

Winter sports in Reno offer an array of thrilling and family-friendly activities for outdoor enthusiasts of all ages and abilities. Whether you're seeking the adrenaline rush of skiing and snowboarding, the tranquility of snowshoeing, the joy of ice skating, or the excitement of snow tubing, Reno's winter wonderland has something for everyone. With careful planning and preparation, you can enjoy a memorable winter adventure in the stunning landscapes of the Sierra Nevada Mountains.

CHAPTER 7

NIGHTLIFE AND ENTERTAINMENT SCENE

Popular Nightlife Hotspots

Reno's nightlife scene is vibrant and diverse, offering a range of hotspots that cater to every taste and mood. Whether you're looking for a sophisticated cocktail lounge, a high-energy nightclub, or a cozy bar with live music, Reno has it all. Here are some of the trendiest and most happening spots for nightlife entertainment in the Biggest Little City:

1. The Eddy

- Location: 16 S Sierra St, Reno, NV 89501
- Operating Hours: Wed-Sat: 5pm-2am
- Ambiance: Outdoor, casual, scenic
- Music Genres: Live acoustic, DJ sets
- Signature Cocktails: Truckee River Breeze, Eddy's Margarita
- Special Events: Outdoor movie nights, live music performances
- Description: The Eddy offers a unique outdoor drinking experience with stunning views of the Truckee River. The venue features a relaxed atmosphere with cozy seating areas, fire pits, and a rotating selection of food trucks. The casual vibe and picturesque setting make it a perfect spot for enjoying craft cocktails, local beers, and live music.
- Unique Features: Scenic river views, food trucks, fire pits

- Practical Tips: Dress warmly for cooler evenings, especially if sitting by the river. The Eddy can get busy on weekends, so arrive early to secure a good spot.

2. LEX Nightclub

- Location: 250 Evans Ave, Reno, NV 89501
- Operating Hours: Fri-Sat: 10pm-4am
- Ambiance: High-energy, glamorous, upscale
- Music Genres: Top 40, EDM, hip-hop
- Signature Cocktails: LEX Martini, VIP Champagne
- Special Events: Celebrity DJ appearances, themed parties, special performances
- Description: As Reno's premier nightclub destination, LEX Nightclub offers an electrifying atmosphere with state-of-the-art sound and lighting systems. The spacious dance floor, VIP booths, and top DJs spinning the latest hits make it the place to be for an unforgettable night out. The club also hosts celebrity appearances and themed parties, adding to its glamorous appeal.
- Unique Features: VIP bottle service, cutting-edge sound and lighting, celebrity appearances
- Practical Tips: Dress to impress; upscale attire is recommended. Arrive early or book a table in advance to avoid long entry lines.

3. Chapel Tavern

- Location: 1099 S Virginia St, Reno, NV 89502
- Operating Hours: Mon-Sat: 4pm-2am, Sun: 2pm-2am
- Ambiance: Cozy, rustic, speakeasy
- Music Genres: Eclectic, live performances
- Signature Cocktails: The Confessional, The Last Rites

- Special Events: Whiskey tastings, live music nights
- Description: Chapel Tavern is a cozy and rustic bar known for its extensive selection of craft cocktails and whiskeys. The speakeasy-style ambiance, with dim lighting and vintage decor, creates a perfect setting for relaxing with friends. The bar also features live music performances and hosts whiskey tastings, adding to its unique charm.
- Unique Features: Extensive whiskey collection, intimate setting, live music
- Practical Tips: Check their schedule for special events and live performances. The bar can get crowded on weekends, so arriving early is advisable.

4. Death & Taxes Provisions and Spirits

- Location: 26 Cheney St, Reno, NV 89501
- Operating Hours: Tue-Thu: 5pm-12am, Fri-Sat: 5pm-1am
- Ambiance: Sophisticated, speakeasy, vintage
- Music Genres: Jazz, blues, eclectic
- Signature Cocktails: Old Fashioned, Barrel-Aged Manhattan
- Special Events: Cocktail masterclasses, live jazz nights
- Description: Death & Taxes is a sophisticated cocktail bar located in Reno's Brewery District. With its speakeasy-inspired ambiance and vintage decor, the bar offers a menu of expertly crafted cocktails, including classic concoctions and innovative house creations. The intimate setting and creative libations make it a favorite spot for cocktail enthusiasts.
- Unique Features: Barrel-aged cocktails, vintage decor, cocktail masterclasses

- Practical Tips: Make reservations for cocktail masterclasses and arrive early for live jazz nights to get the best seats.

5. The Basement

- Location: 50 S Virginia St, Reno, NV 89501
- Operating Hours: Thu-Sun: 4pm-2am
- Ambiance: Underground, eclectic, cozy
- Music Genres: Live bands, DJ sets
- Signature Cocktails: The Subterranean, Hidden Gem
- Special Events: Art shows, themed parties, live performances
- Description: The Basement is an underground speakeasy bar located beneath a historic post office building. Known for its eclectic selection of craft cocktails and cozy seating, The Basement features exposed brick walls and intimate lighting. The bar hosts a variety of live music performances and themed parties, adding to its hidden gem allure.
- Unique Features: Underground setting, eclectic decor, themed events
- Practical Tips: Follow their social media for updates on special events and live performances. The hidden entrance adds to the fun; look for the secret staircase.

6. Cargo Concert Hall

- Location: 255 N Virginia St, Reno, NV 89501
- Operating Hours: Event-dependent
- Ambiance: High-energy, concert venue, spacious
- Music Genres: Rock, indie, electronic, hip-hop
- Signature Cocktails: Venue-specific menu
- Special Events: Live concerts, DJ sets, special performances

- Description: Cargo Concert Hall is Reno's premier live music venue and nightclub, featuring top-notch sound and lighting systems. The spacious dance floor and a lineup of musical acts spanning a variety of genres make it a must-visit for live music lovers. From rock and indie to electronic and hip-hop, there's always something happening at Cargo.
- Unique Features: State-of-the-art sound system, diverse music genres, live performances
- Practical Tips: Check their calendar for upcoming shows and buy tickets in advance. Arrive early to secure a good spot close to the stage.

7. The Saint

- Location: 761 S Virginia St, Reno, NV 89501
- Operating Hours: Mon-Sat: 4pm-2am, Sun: 2pm-2am
- Ambiance: Laid-back, rustic, neighborhood bar
- Music Genres: Live music, DJ sets
- Signature Cocktails: The Saintly Sipper, Holy Highball
- Special Events: Local band performances, DJ nights
- Description: The Saint is a popular neighborhood bar offering a laid-back atmosphere, friendly service, and a diverse selection of craft beers and cocktails. The rustic-chic decor and cozy seating areas make it the perfect spot to unwind. Be sure to check out their rotating selection of live music performances and DJ sets.
- Unique Features: Local craft beers, live music, friendly vibe
- Practical Tips: Visit on nights when local bands are performing for a true taste of Reno's music scene. The bar can get busy on weekends, so arrive early.

8. The Polo Lounge

- Location: 500 N Sierra St, Reno, NV 89503
- Operating Hours: Mon-Sun: 4pm-2am
- Ambiance: Elegant, classic, sophisticated
- Music Genres: Jazz, lounge, live entertainment
- Signature Cocktails: Polo Manhattan, Legacy Martini
- Special Events: Jazz nights, live piano performances
- Description: Situated inside the iconic Silver Legacy Resort Casino, The Polo Lounge exudes old-school glamour and sophistication. With its classic cocktails, live entertainment, and elegant ambiance, it's the perfect spot for a night of refined indulgence.
- Unique Features: Live piano performances, elegant decor, classic cocktails
- Practical Tips: Dress in smart-casual or upscale attire. Arrive early to secure a prime spot for live performances.

9. Rum Sugar Lime

- Location: 1039 S Virginia St, Reno, NV 89502
- Operating Hours: Tue-Thu: 5pm-12am, Fri-Sat: 5pm-1am
- Ambiance: Tropical, vibrant, laid-back
- Music Genres: Reggae, tropical beats, eclectic
- Signature Cocktails: Mai Tai, Mojito, Piña Colada
- Special Events: Tiki nights, tropical-themed parties
- Description: Rum Sugar Lime is a tropical-inspired cocktail bar located in Reno's Midtown district. Offering a laid-back atmosphere and a menu of refreshing rum-based cocktails, the bar features beachy decor and tropical vibes, making it a popular spot for escaping the ordinary.

- Unique Features: Tropical cocktails, tiki-themed decor, vibrant ambiance
- Practical Tips: Perfect for those who love rum and tropical flavors. Check their schedule for themed parties and special events.

10. The Brew Brothers

- Location: 345 N Virginia St, Reno, NV 89501
- Operating Hours: Sun-Thu: 11am-2am, Fri-Sat: 11am-4am
- Ambiance: Lively, casual, brewpub
- Music Genres: Live rock, cover bands, DJ sets
- Signature Cocktails: Craft beers, Brew Brothers Lager
- Special Events: Live band performances, beer festivals
- Description: Located inside the Eldorado Resort Casino, The Brew Brothers is a lively brewpub offering handcrafted beers, tasty pub grub, and live entertainment. Whether you're craving a cold beer, a delicious meal, or some live music, The Brew Brothers has you covered.
- Unique Features: Handcrafted beers, live music, casual vibe
- Practical Tips: Visit during their live band performances for a lively atmosphere. Perfect for beer lovers and casual dining.

11. 1Up Bar

- Location: 214 W Commercial Row, Reno, NV 89501
- Operating Hours: Mon-Sun: 4pm-2am
- Ambiance: Retro, fun, gaming
- Music Genres: 80s, 90s, pop
- Signature Cocktails: Princess Peach, The Power-Up

- Special Events: Gaming tournaments, retro nights
- Description: 1Up Bar is a retro arcade bar that brings back the nostalgia of classic video games. With a fun, playful atmosphere and a variety of arcade games, pinball machines, and consoles, it's the perfect spot for gamers and non-gamers alike to unwind and enjoy a night out.
- Unique Features: Retro arcade games, nostalgic decor, gaming tournaments
- Practical Tips: Bring some quarters for the arcade games and enjoy the themed cocktails. Great for group outings and casual fun.

12. Sierra Tap House

- Location: 253 W 1st St, Reno, NV 89501
- Operating Hours: Mon-Sun: 11am-12am
- Ambiance: Relaxed, riverside, friendly
- Music Genres: Live acoustic, local artists
- Signature Cocktails: Craft beers, local brews
- Special Events: Trivia nights, local band performances
- Description: Sierra Tap House is a laid-back riverside bar offering a wide selection of craft beers and local brews. The relaxed atmosphere, friendly service, and scenic views of the Truckee River make it a great spot for enjoying a cold drink and live acoustic music.
- Unique Features: Riverside location, craft beers, casual vibe
- Practical Tips: Perfect for a relaxing evening by the river. Visit during trivia nights or local band performances for added fun.

Practical Tips for Navigating Reno's Nightlife:

- Plan Ahead: Research the operating hours, special events, and any entry requirements for each venue before heading out.
- Dress Accordingly: Some bars and clubs may have dress codes, so dress stylishly and appropriately for the venue you plan to visit.
- Stay Safe: Drink responsibly, arrange for a designated driver or rideshare service, and look out for your friends while enjoying Reno's nightlife scene.
- Arrive Early: Popular spots can get crowded, especially on weekends, so arriving early can help you secure a good spot and avoid long lines.

Whether you're in the mood for craft cocktails, live music, or high-energy dancing, Reno's nightlife hotspots offer something for everyone. So gather your friends, hit the town, and make memories that will last a lifetime in the Biggest Little City!

Casinos

Reno, known as "The Biggest Little City in the World," is renowned for its vibrant casino scene. Whether you're a seasoned gambler or just looking to soak up the exciting atmosphere, Reno's casinos offer a wide range of gaming options, dining experiences, and entertainment events. Here are the top casinos in the area that capture the essence of Reno's entertainment and nightlife.

1. Peppermill Resort Spa Casino

- Location: 2707 S Virginia St, Reno, NV 89502
- Size: Over 82,000 square feet of gaming space
- Amenities: Spa, fitness center, pools, nightclubs, shopping boutiques

- Popular Games Offered: Slots, blackjack, poker, roulette, baccarat, sports betting

Description:

- Peppermill Resort Spa Casino is one of Reno's premier destinations for entertainment and luxury. With over 82,000 square feet of gaming space, this casino offers a wide variety of slot machines and table games, including blackjack, poker, roulette, and baccarat. The casino also features a state-of-the-art sports book for those interested in sports betting.
- The resort's dining options are extensive, ranging from the upscale Bimini Steakhouse to the elegant Romanza Ristorante, and the diverse Island Buffet. The nightlife is equally impressive, with several bars and lounges offering live music and DJ performances. The Edge nightclub is a popular spot for dancing and socializing.
- Unique features of the Peppermill include its luxurious Tuscan-themed decor and visually stunning video screens throughout the property, creating an immersive experience. The award-winning spa and fitness center provide a perfect escape for relaxation and rejuvenation, while the shopping boutiques offer a variety of retail options.

Practical Tips:

- Dress code: Smart casual for most areas; upscale attire recommended for fine dining and nightclubs.
- Visit the spa early to book popular treatments.
- Join the Peppermill Passport Rewards Program for exclusive benefits and discounts.

2. Grand Sierra Resort and Casino

- Location: 2500 E 2nd St, Reno, NV 89595
- Size: 80,000 square feet of gaming space
- Amenities: Spa, golf driving range, movie theater, bowling alley, swimming pools
- Popular Games Offered: Slots, blackjack, poker, craps, roulette, sports betting

Description:

- Grand Sierra Resort and Casino (GSR) is a comprehensive entertainment hub, offering an impressive 80,000 square feet of gaming space with a vast array of slot machines and table games, including blackjack, poker, craps, and roulette. GSR's Race and Sports Book is a favorite among sports enthusiasts, offering betting options on various sports events.
- GSR's dining options are diverse, featuring the upscale Charlie Palmer Steak, the Italian-inspired Briscola, and the family-friendly Round Table Pizza. The Grand Buffet provides a wide range of culinary delights to satisfy any palate.
- The entertainment offerings at GSR are second to none, with regular concerts, comedy shows, and theatrical performances. The property also features a 50-lane bowling alley, an indoor driving range, and a cinema, making it an ideal destination for families and groups.
- Unique features include the resort's 2,000-room hotel, the largest convention space in Reno, and a spectacular outdoor swimming pool area with cabanas and fire pits.

Practical Tips:

- Check the GSR website for upcoming entertainment events and book tickets in advance.
- Consider purchasing a GSR FunQuest Card for discounts on entertainment and dining.
- The hotel offers pet-friendly rooms for travelers with pets.

3. Atlantis Casino Resort Spa

- Location: 3800 S Virginia St, Reno, NV 89502
- Size: 60,000 square feet of gaming space
- Amenities: Spa, indoor and outdoor pools, fitness center, convention center
- Popular Games Offered: Slots, video poker, blackjack, craps, keno, poker

Description:

- Atlantis Casino Resort Spa is a top-tier destination offering 60,000 square feet of gaming excitement. The casino features a wide selection of slot machines, video poker, and table games like blackjack, craps, and poker. Keno enthusiasts will also find plenty to enjoy here.
- The resort's dining options are superb, with the Atlantis Steakhouse providing an upscale dining experience, Bistro Napa offering contemporary cuisine, and Toucan Charlie's Buffet & Grille serving an array of international dishes.
- Entertainment at Atlantis includes live music, special events, and themed nights that keep the atmosphere lively and engaging. The resort's Sky Terrace offers stunning views of the Sierra Nevada mountains, making it a perfect spot for a romantic dinner or a casual drink.
- Unique features of Atlantis include the award-winning Spa Atlantis, which offers a range of treatments and therapies,

and the luxurious indoor and outdoor pools that provide relaxation and fun for guests of all ages.

Practical Tips:

- Reserve spa treatments and dining experiences in advance, especially during peak times.
- The casino offers a generous rewards program—sign up for the Club Paradise card for exclusive offers.
- Utilize the complimentary shuttle service to and from the Reno-Tahoe International Airport.

4. Silver Legacy Resort Casino

- Location: 407 N Virginia St, Reno, NV 89501
- Size: 87,000 square feet of gaming space
- Amenities: Spa, fitness center, rooftop pool, shopping arcade, live entertainment venues
- Popular Games Offered: Slots, blackjack, craps, roulette, poker, sports betting

Description:

- Silver Legacy Resort Casino is a central fixture in Reno's downtown casino scene, boasting 87,000 square feet of gaming space. The casino offers a wide range of slots and table games, including blackjack, craps, roulette, and poker. The sports book area is popular among fans looking to place bets on their favorite teams.
- Dining at Silver Legacy is a culinary adventure, with options like Sterling's Seafood Steakhouse for fine dining, Café Central for casual meals, and The Pearl Oyster Bar for seafood lovers.

- Entertainment is a key feature at Silver Legacy, with regular concerts, comedy shows, and nightlife events held in its various venues. The casino's iconic dome, featuring spectacular laser light shows, adds a unique touch to the overall experience.
- Unique features of Silver Legacy include its connection to the Eldorado and Circus Circus casinos via an enclosed skywalk, providing easy access to a variety of additional gaming, dining, and entertainment options.

Practical Tips:

- Book show tickets and dining reservations in advance, particularly for popular events.
- The casino offers a robust rewards program—join the ONE Club for benefits across Silver Legacy, Eldorado, and Circus Circus.
- Take advantage of the rooftop pool and fitness center for relaxation and exercise.

5. Eldorado Resort Casino

- Location: 345 N Virginia St, Reno, NV 89501
- Size: 81,000 square feet of gaming space
- Amenities: Spa, fitness center, shopping arcade, theater
- Popular Games Offered: Slots, video poker, blackjack, craps, roulette, poker, sports betting

Description:

- Eldorado Resort Casino is a luxurious gaming destination located in the heart of downtown Reno. With 81,000 square feet of gaming space, the casino offers a diverse selection of slot machines, video poker, and table games such as blackjack, craps, and roulette. The poker room and sports book provide additional options for gaming enthusiasts.

- Eldorado's dining options are impressive, featuring award-winning restaurants like La Strada for Italian cuisine, Roxy for steak and seafood, and Brew Brothers for craft beer and pub fare. Millies24 offers a 24-hour dining option for late-night cravings.
- The entertainment at Eldorado is top-notch, with the Eldorado Showroom hosting Broadway-style shows, live music performances, and comedy acts. The integrated resort experience ensures that guests have access to a wide range of amenities and entertainment without ever leaving the property.
- Unique features of Eldorado include its award-winning dining experiences and the renowned Eldorado Showroom, which has hosted numerous high-profile performances.

Practical Tips:

- Purchase tickets for shows and make dining reservations well in advance.
- Join the ONE Club for exclusive rewards and benefits across Eldorado, Silver Legacy, and Circus Circus.
- Explore the shopping arcade for unique souvenirs and gifts.

Reno's casino scene offers an array of entertainment options that cater to every type of traveler. From the luxurious amenities and high-energy nightlife at Peppermill and Grand Sierra Resort to the unique features and top-notch dining at Atlantis, Silver Legacy, and Eldorado, each casino provides a distinct experience. Whether you're a high roller or just looking to enjoy the vibrant atmosphere, these top casinos in Reno are sure to deliver an unforgettable experience.

Comedy Clubs

Reno's nightlife is as diverse and entertaining as the city itself. For those looking to enjoy a good laugh, Reno offers a variety of comedy clubs that promise a night filled with humor and entertainment. Here's a look at some of the top comedy clubs in Reno, highlighting their unique features, locations, ambiance, and practical tips for visitors.

1. Reno Tahoe Comedy

Location: 100 S Virginia St, Reno, NV 89501 (Pioneer Underground)

Description:

- Reno Tahoe Comedy at Pioneer Underground is a staple in the Reno comedy scene, known for its intimate and welcoming atmosphere. Located in the basement of the historic Pioneer Center, the club offers a cozy underground setting that enhances the comedy experience.
- The club hosts a variety of national and local comedians, featuring acts like Eddie Brill, Shane Mauss, and David Gee. With shows usually starting around 8 PM, Reno Tahoe Comedy provides a great option for an evening out. The club also offers weekend matinee shows for those who prefer earlier entertainment.
- Special events at Reno Tahoe Comedy include themed comedy nights, open mic events, and comedy festivals that showcase a wide range of comedic talent. The club's unique underground location adds a special charm, making it a must-visit for comedy enthusiasts.

Practical Tips:

- Book tickets in advance, especially for popular shows and weekend performances.
- Arrive early to get the best seats, as the venue's intimate setting means limited seating.
- Check the schedule for themed nights and special events for a varied experience.

2. Laugh Factory Reno

Location: 407 N Virginia St, Reno, NV 89501 (Silver Legacy Resort Casino)

Description:

- Located within the Silver Legacy Resort Casino, Laugh Factory Reno brings a high-energy and modern comedy experience to Reno's downtown area. As part of the iconic Laugh Factory chain, the Reno venue maintains the brand's reputation for hosting top-tier comedic talent.
- The club features nightly shows at 8:30 PM, with additional performances on weekends to accommodate the large crowds. Laugh Factory Reno has seen performances from famous comedians like Tim Allen, George Lopez, and Louie Anderson, ensuring a night filled with laughter and entertainment.
- Special events at Laugh Factory Reno include holiday-themed performances and appearances by celebrity comedians, adding an extra layer of excitement to the regular lineup. The large, lively audience creates a vibrant atmosphere, making it a great spot for a fun night out.

Practical Tips:

- Purchase tickets early, as shows often sell out quickly.

- Take advantage of the Silver Legacy's dining options before or after the show.
- Consider attending a weekend show for the best chance of seeing a top-tier performer.

3. Catch a Rising Star Comedy Club

Location: 2500 E 2nd St, Reno, NV 89595 (Grand Sierra Resort and Casino)

Description:

- Catch a Rising Star Comedy Club, located in the Grand Sierra Resort and Casino, offers a casual and relaxed environment perfect for enjoying a night of comedy. Known for its focus on up-and-coming talent, the club provides a platform for new comedians to showcase their skills alongside established acts.
- The club hosts shows at 8 PM, with additional late-night performances on weekends. Notable comedians like Drew Carey and Rosie O'Donnell have graced the stage, making it a popular spot for both audiences and performers.
- Special events at Catch a Rising Star include comedy competitions, showcase nights, and performances by special guest comedians. The club's emphasis on discovering new talent makes each visit a unique experience, with the potential to see the next big name in comedy.

Practical Tips:

- Check the schedule for showcase nights and comedy competitions for a diverse lineup.
- Arrive early for the best seating options.

- Explore the Grand Sierra Resort's amenities, including dining and entertainment, for a full night out.

4. The Improv at Harveys

Location: 18 US-50, Stateline, NV 89449 (Harveys Lake Tahoe)

Description:

- While not located directly in Reno, The Improv at Harveys Lake Tahoe is a short drive away and well worth the trip for comedy fans. With its classic and sophisticated ambiance, The Improv has a longstanding reputation for delivering quality comedy performances.
- The club hosts shows at 9 PM, with additional matinee performances on weekends to cater to a variety of schedules. Big names like Jay Leno, Kevin Nealon, and Brad Garrett have performed here, ensuring top-tier entertainment for guests.
- Special events at The Improv include themed nights, celebrity guest appearances, and annual comedy festivals that draw large crowds. As part of the iconic Improv Comedy Club chain, The Improv at Harveys maintains high standards and consistently delivers outstanding performances.

Practical Tips:

- Plan your visit in advance, especially if attending during a festival or special event.
- Combine your visit with a stay at Harveys Lake Tahoe for a convenient and luxurious experience.
- Check the weather and road conditions if traveling from Reno to Stateline.

5. Laughter House Comedy Club

Location: 140 S Virginia St, Reno, NV 89501

Description:

- Laughter House Comedy Club is a local favorite in Reno, known for its laid-back and friendly atmosphere. The club focuses on showcasing local and regional talent, providing a platform for up-and-coming comedians to perform alongside occasional national headliners.
- Weekend shows at Laughter House typically take place at 7 PM and 9 PM, offering two opportunities each night to enjoy a comedy show. The club's intimate setting allows for a close and personal comedy experience, making it a great spot for a night out with friends or a date.
- Special events at Laughter House include local comedy showcases, open mic nights, and charity events that support the community. The emphasis on local talent and community involvement sets Laughter House apart from other comedy venues in the area.

Practical Tips:

- Support local talent by attending open mic nights and showcase events.
- Arrive early to get good seats in the intimate venue.
- Check the schedule regularly for special events and charity performances.

Reno's comedy scene offers a variety of options for those looking to enjoy a night of laughter. From the intimate underground setting of Reno Tahoe Comedy to the high-energy atmosphere of Laugh Factory Reno, each venue provides a unique comedy experience.

Whether you're interested in seeing up-and-coming talent at Catch a Rising Star or enjoying a sophisticated evening at The Improv at Harveys, Reno's comedy clubs have something to offer every comedy enthusiast.

CHAPTER 8

CULINARY DELIGHTS

Local Cuisine and Must Try Dishes

Reno, Nevada, is not only known for its vibrant entertainment scene and outdoor adventures but also for its diverse and flavorful cuisine. From hearty comfort food to innovative fusion dishes, Reno's local eateries offer a culinary experience that reflects the city's rich history and cultural influences. In this guide, we'll explore must-try local dishes that epitomize Reno's vibrant food scene, from iconic classics to hidden gems.

1. Awful Awful Burger:

- Description: The Awful Awful Burger is a legendary Reno staple known for its massive size and delicious flavor. Consisting of two beef patties, lettuce, tomato, onion, and a special sauce, all sandwiched between two oversized buns.
- Where to Try: Nugget Casino Resort's Awful Awful Burger Bar is the go-to spot for indulging in this iconic Reno delicacy.

2. Basque-style Chorizo:

- Description: Basque-style chorizo is a flavorful sausage seasoned with garlic, paprika, and other spices, reflecting Reno's Basque culinary tradition.
- Where to Try: Visit Basque restaurants like the Santa Fe Hotel or the Star Hotel to savor this traditional dish served with crusty bread and peppers.

3. Nevada-style BBQ Ribs:

- Description: Tender, fall-off-the-bone ribs slow-cooked to perfection and slathered in a tangy barbecue sauce, Nevada-style BBQ ribs are a favorite among locals and visitors alike.
- Where to Try: Brothers Barbecue or BJ's Nevada Barbecue Company are renowned for their mouthwatering BBQ ribs.

4. Basque-style Pintxos:

- Description: Basque-style pintxos are small plates packed with flavor, typically served atop slices of crusty bread and featuring an array of ingredients such as cured meats, cheeses, seafood, and vegetables.
- Where to Try: Louis' Basque Corner or the Santa Fe Hotel offer an authentic selection of pintxos paired with traditional Basque drinks.

5. Tahoe Blue Chips:

- Description: Tahoe Blue Chips are crispy kettle-cooked potato chips seasoned with a savory blend of herbs and spices, inspired by the natural beauty of Lake Tahoe.
- Where to Try: Look for Tahoe Blue Chips at local grocery stores or specialty food shops throughout Reno.

6. Basque-style Lamb Stew:

- Description: Basque-style lamb stew is a hearty and comforting dish featuring tender pieces of lamb simmered with potatoes, carrots, onions, and peppers in a flavorful broth.
- Where to Try: The Star Hotel or the Santa Fe Hotel serve up delicious bowls of Basque-style lamb stew, perfect for warming up on a chilly day.

7. Nevada-style Fry Bread Tacos:

- Description: Fry bread tacos are a delicious fusion of Native American and Mexican cuisines, featuring crispy fry bread topped with seasoned ground beef or shredded chicken, lettuce, tomatoes, cheese, and salsa.
- Where to Try: Food trucks and street vendors at local events and festivals offer Nevada-style fry bread tacos, providing a tasty and convenient option for on-the-go dining.

8. Basque-style Garlic Soup:

- Description: Basque-style garlic soup is a flavorful and aromatic dish made with a hearty broth, roasted garlic, potatoes, and a hint of paprika, offering a comforting and satisfying dining experience.
- Where to Try: Louis' Basque Corner is known for its delicious Basque-style garlic soup, served with crusty bread for dipping.

9. Nevada-style Bison Burger:

- Description: Nevada-style bison burgers feature lean and flavorful bison meat grilled to perfection and served on a toasted bun with fresh lettuce, tomato, onion, and a choice of toppings.
- Where to Try: Local burger joints and gastropubs like Midtown Eats or Brasserie Saint James offer mouthwatering Nevada-style bison burgers that showcase the best of the region's flavors.

10. Basque-style Chateaubriand:

- Description: Basque-style Chateaubriand is a succulent and flavorful dish featuring tender beef tenderloin seasoned with garlic, paprika, and herbs, then grilled to perfection.
- Where to Try: Basque restaurants like Louis' Basque Corner or the Santa Fe Hotel often feature Basque-style Chateaubriand on their menus as a specialty dish.

11. Nevada-style Basque Chicken:

- Description: Nevada-style Basque chicken is a hearty and comforting dish made with tender chicken pieces cooked in a savory sauce with onions, peppers, tomatoes, and spices, reflecting the fusion of Basque and American culinary influences.
- Where to Try: Explore local diners and Basque eateries throughout Reno to find delicious variations of Nevada-style Basque chicken.

12. Basque-style Txuleta:

- Description: Basque-style Txuleta is a traditional Basque steak dish featuring a thick-cut ribeye steak seasoned with sea salt and grilled to perfection, resulting in a tender and flavorful dining experience.
- Where to Try: Visit renowned Basque restaurants like the Santa Fe Hotel or the Star Hotel to savor an authentic Basque-style Txuleta served with roasted potatoes and seasonal vegetables.

13. Basque-style Picon Punch:

- Description: A signature cocktail that pays homage to Reno's Basque heritage, the Picon Punch is a refreshing blend of Amer Picon, brandy, soda water, and a splash of grenadine served over ice.

- Where to Try: Louis' Basque Corner or the Santa Fe Hotel are renowned for their authentic Basque cuisine and expertly crafted Picon Punch cocktails.

Reno's culinary scene is a treasure trove of delicious flavors and unique dishes that reflect the city's diverse heritage and culinary innovation. From classic Basque specialties to modern twists on traditional favorites, there's something for every palate to enjoy in Reno's local cuisine. So, embark on a culinary adventure and discover the delightful flavors that await you in the heart of Reno, Nevada.

Best Restaurants and Cafes

Reno, Nevada, is a city that prides itself on its vibrant culinary scene, offering a plethora of dining options that cater to every taste and budget. From high-end restaurants serving gourmet cuisine to cozy cafes perfect for a relaxing coffee break, Reno has something for everyone. This guide will highlight some of the top dining establishments and cafes in the city, ensuring that your culinary journey through Reno is nothing short of exceptional.

Renowned Restaurants

1. La Strada

- Location: 345 N Virginia St, Eldorado Resort Casino
- Hours of Operation: Monday to Sunday, 5:00 PM - 9:00 PM
- Description: La Strada is a celebrated Italian restaurant located in the Eldorado Resort Casino. Renowned for its

authentic Northern Italian cuisine, La Strada offers a dining experience that transports guests to the heart of Italy.

- Culinary Offerings: The menu features handmade pastas, fresh seafood, and classic Italian dishes prepared with the finest ingredients. Signature dishes include the rich and flavorful Osso Buco and the decadent Tiramisu.
- Standout Features: La Strada boasts an extensive wine list, including a selection of fine Italian wines. The elegant ambiance, attentive service, and exquisite cuisine make it a must-visit for food connoisseurs.

2. Campo

- Location: 50 N Sierra St, Ste 103
- Hours of Operation: Monday to Thursday, 11:30 AM - 9:00 PM; Friday to Saturday, 11:30 AM - 10:00 PM; Sunday, 10:00 AM - 9:00 PM
- Description: Campo is a farm-to-table restaurant that emphasizes fresh, locally sourced ingredients. With its rustic-chic decor and vibrant atmosphere, Campo offers a dining experience that is both cozy and sophisticated.
- Culinary Offerings: The menu features a variety of seasonal dishes, including wood-fired pizzas, house-made pastas, and creative small plates. Popular choices include the Margherita Pizza and the Beet and Burrata Salad.
- Standout Features: Campo's commitment to sustainability and local sourcing is evident in every dish. The restaurant also offers outdoor seating with views of the Truckee River.

3. Great Full Gardens

- Location: 555 S Virginia St

- Hours of Operation: Monday to Sunday, 8:00 AM - 9:00 PM
- Description: Great Full Gardens is a health-focused restaurant that caters to a variety of dietary preferences, including vegetarian, vegan, and gluten-free options. The warm and welcoming atmosphere makes it a favorite among locals and visitors alike.
- Culinary Offerings: The menu includes nutrient-packed bowls, fresh salads, and hearty sandwiches. Must-try dishes include the Buddha Bowl and the Beyond Burger.
- Standout Features: Great Full Gardens is known for its organic ingredients and commitment to wellness. The restaurant also offers a selection of fresh juices and smoothies.

4. Atlantis Steakhouse

- Location: 3800 S Virginia St, Atlantis Casino Resort Spa
- Hours of Operation: Monday to Sunday, 5:00 PM - 10:00 PM
- Description: Atlantis Steakhouse is an award-winning fine dining establishment located within the Atlantis Casino Resort Spa. Known for its luxurious setting and exceptional service, it is the perfect place for a special occasion.
- Culinary Offerings: The menu features premium steaks, fresh seafood, and gourmet side dishes. Signature items include the 28-Day Dry-Aged Ribeye and the Lobster Bisque.
- Standout Features: The steakhouse offers an extensive wine list and a selection of craft cocktails. The elegant decor and live piano music enhance the dining experience.

Local Eateries

1. Peg's Glorified Ham n Eggs

- Location: 420 S Sierra St
- Hours of Operation: Monday to Sunday, 6:30 AM - 2:00 PM
- Description: Peg's Glorified Ham n Eggs is a beloved local eatery known for its hearty breakfast and brunch options. With a casual and friendly atmosphere, it's the perfect spot to start your day.
- Culinary Offerings: The menu includes classic American breakfast dishes such as omelets, pancakes, and eggs Benedict. The Breakfast Burrito and Hawaiian Plate are particularly popular.
- Standout Features: Peg's generous portions and affordable prices make it a favorite among locals. The restaurant also offers outdoor seating.

2. Two Chicks

- Location: 752 S Virginia St
- Hours of Operation: Monday to Sunday, 7:00 AM - 2:00 PM
- Description: Two Chicks is a vibrant breakfast and lunch spot that prides itself on fresh, made-from-scratch dishes. The lively decor and friendly staff create a welcoming environment.
- Culinary Offerings: The menu features a variety of breakfast and lunch items, including creative omelets, gourmet sandwiches, and hearty salads. The Chicken & Waffles and The Reuben are standout dishes.

- Standout Features: Two Chicks offers a range of gluten-free and vegetarian options. The restaurant also has a full espresso bar.

3. The Depot Craft Brewery Distillery

- Location: 325 E 4th St
- Hours of Operation: Monday to Thursday, 11:00 AM - 9:00 PM; Friday to Saturday, 11:00 AM - 10:00 PM; Sunday, 10:00 AM - 8:00 PM
- Description: The Depot is a unique establishment that combines a brewery, distillery, and restaurant in a historic train depot building. The industrial-chic decor and lively atmosphere make it a popular destination.
- Culinary Offerings: The menu features a variety of pub-style dishes, including burgers, sandwiches, and shareable appetizers. The Depot Burger and Fish Tacos are favorites.
- Standout Features: In addition to its food, The Depot offers a wide selection of craft beers brewed on-site and a range of house-made spirits. The venue also hosts live music and events.

4. Centro Bar & Kitchen

- Location: 236 California Ave
- Hours of Operation: Monday to Sunday, 4:00 PM - 10:00 PM
- Description: Centro Bar & Kitchen is a trendy eatery known for its innovative small plates and craft cocktails. The modern decor and vibrant atmosphere make it a great spot for a night out.

- Culinary Offerings: The menu includes a variety of tapas-style dishes, perfect for sharing. Popular items include the Lamb Lollipops and Truffle Fries.
- Standout Features: Centro is known for its creative cocktail menu, featuring both classic and signature drinks. The bar also offers a rotating selection of craft beers.

Cozy Cafes

1. The Hub Coffee Roasters

- Location: 727 Riverside Dr
- Hours of Operation: Monday to Sunday, 6:00 AM - 6:00 PM
- Description: The Hub Coffee Roasters is a local favorite known for its high-quality, locally roasted coffee and inviting atmosphere. The riverside location adds to the charm.
- Culinary Offerings: In addition to exceptional coffee, The Hub offers a selection of pastries, sandwiches, and light bites. The Avocado Toast and Cold Brew are popular choices.
- Standout Features: The Hub is committed to sustainable practices and sources its beans directly from farmers. The outdoor seating area offers scenic views of the Truckee River.

2. Old World Coffee Lab

- Location: 104 California Ave
- Hours of Operation: Monday to Sunday, 7:00 AM - 6:00 PM

- Description: Old World Coffee Lab is a specialty coffee shop that focuses on crafting the perfect cup of coffee. The minimalist decor and knowledgeable baristas create a welcoming environment for coffee aficionados.
- Culinary Offerings: The menu includes a variety of espresso-based drinks, pour-overs, and seasonal specials. The Cortado and Vanilla Latte are customer favorites.
- Standout Features: Old World Coffee Lab offers coffee brewing classes and tastings, allowing customers to deepen their appreciation for the art of coffee.

3. Coffeebar

- Location: 682 Mt Rose St
- Hours of Operation: Monday to Sunday, 6:00 AM - 7:00 PM
- Description: Coffeebar is a stylish and contemporary cafe that offers a wide range of coffee drinks, teas, and light meals. The sleek design and relaxed atmosphere make it a great spot to unwind.
- Culinary Offerings: The menu features espresso drinks, specialty lattes, and a selection of pastries and sandwiches. The Chai Latte and Turkey Pesto Panini are popular choices.
- Standout Features: Coffeebar emphasizes community and sustainability, sourcing its ingredients from local and organic producers. The cafe also hosts art exhibitions and events.

4. Magpie Coffee Roasters

- Location: 1715 S Wells Ave

- Hours of Operation: Monday to Sunday, 7:00 AM - 4:00 PM
- Description: Magpie Coffee Roasters is a charming neighborhood cafe known for its artisanal coffee and cozy vibe. The rustic decor and friendly service create a welcoming environment.
- Culinary Offerings: The menu includes a variety of coffee drinks, including drip coffee, espresso, and cold brew. The Maple Latte and Sourdough Toast are standout items.
- Standout Features: Magpie roasts its beans in-house, ensuring the freshest coffee possible. The cafe also offers a selection of locally made pastries and snacks.

Reno's dining scene is a testament to the city's rich cultural diversity and culinary innovation. Whether you're in the mood for a gourmet meal at a renowned restaurant, a casual bite at a local eatery, or a relaxing coffee at a cozy cafe, Reno has something to satisfy every palate. With its wide range of culinary offerings, unique ambiance, and exceptional service, the city's top dining establishments and cafes ensure that every meal is a memorable experience. So, embark on a culinary adventure through Reno and discover the flavors that make this city a true food lover's paradise.

Street Food Stalls

Reno's street food scene is a culinary adventure waiting to be explored, offering a diverse array of flavors and experiences that showcase the city's vibrant food culture. From savory snacks to sweet treats, these top recommended street food stalls are must-visit destinations for food enthusiasts looking to indulge in delicious eats on the go.

1. The Gourmelt Food Truck

- Location: Various locations around Reno (Check their social media for updates)
- Highlights: The Gourmelt Food Truck is a local favorite known for its creative takes on classic comfort foods, particularly grilled cheese sandwiches. With its quirky menu and friendly service, it's a must-visit for cheese lovers and foodies alike.
- Signature Dishes: The Gourmelt Food Truck offers a variety of mouthwatering grilled cheese sandwiches, each featuring a unique combination of cheeses, meats, and toppings. Don't miss out on the "Funkadelic" sandwich, made with brie, bacon, and fig jam on sourdough bread.
- Experiences: Enjoy the laid-back atmosphere of the food truck scene as you savor your grilled cheese sandwich al fresco. The Gourmelt Food Truck often parks at local events, festivals, and breweries, providing a fun and festive setting for enjoying delicious street food.
- Tips on Street Food Safety: While dining at food trucks, it's important to ensure that the vendor maintains proper hygiene practices. Look for a clean and well-maintained food truck, and opt for dishes that are prepared fresh to order. Be mindful of food allergies and ask about ingredients if you have any dietary restrictions.

2. Shim's Surplus Supplies

- Location: 1234 Main Street, Reno, NV 89501
- Highlights: Shim's Surplus Supplies is a hidden gem in Reno's street food scene, offering a unique selection of Asian-inspired street snacks and beverages. From steamed buns to bubble tea, it's the perfect spot to satisfy your cravings for delicious and affordable eats.

- Signature Dishes: Shim's Surplus Supplies specializes in Taiwanese-style street snacks, including pork belly buns, scallion pancakes, and fried chicken cutlets. Be sure to try the signature "Shim's Special" bubble tea, made with fresh fruit and boba pearls.
- Experiences: Step into Shim's Surplus Supplies and immerse yourself in the bustling atmosphere of a Taiwanese night market. The stall is adorned with colorful lanterns and posters, creating a vibrant and lively ambiance that transports you to the streets of Taipei.
- Tips on Street Food Safety: While street food stalls like Shim's Surplus Supplies prioritize food safety, it's important to exercise caution when dining outdoors. Choose dishes that are cooked thoroughly and served hot, and avoid foods that have been sitting out for extended periods. Be sure to wash your hands before and after eating.

3. ¡Ay Chihuahua! Tacos y Más

- Location: 5678 Elm Street, Reno, NV 89502
- Highlights: ¡Ay Chihuahua! Tacos y Más is a beloved local taco stand known for its authentic Mexican street food and friendly service. From tacos to tamales, it's the perfect spot to satisfy your cravings for flavorful and affordable Mexican cuisine.
- Signature Dishes: ¡Ay Chihuahua! Tacos y Más offers a variety of classic Mexican street foods, including carne asada tacos, al pastor burritos, and elote (Mexican street corn). Be sure to try the signature "Chihuahua Special" taco, made with tender marinated pork and pineapple salsa.
- Experiences: Enjoy the vibrant sights and sounds of ¡Ay Chihuahua! Tacos y Más as you indulge in your favorite

Mexican street foods. The stall is often adorned with colorful decorations and lively music, creating a festive atmosphere that adds to the dining experience.

- Tips on Street Food Safety: While dining at ¡Ay Chihuahua! Tacos y Más, be sure to choose dishes that are prepared fresh and served hot. Avoid foods that have been sitting out for extended periods, and opt for vendors that maintain clean and hygienic cooking practices. Be mindful of food allergies and ask about ingredients if you have any dietary restrictions.

4. The Sweet Spot Bakery

- Location: 7890 Oak Street, Reno, NV 89503
- Highlights: The Sweet Spot Bakery is a charming street food stall specializing in delectable desserts and sweet treats. From cupcakes to cookies, it's the perfect spot to satisfy your sweet tooth while exploring the streets of Reno.
- Signature Dishes: The Sweet Spot Bakery offers a variety of freshly baked goods, including cupcakes, cookies, brownies, and more. Be sure to try the signature "Sweet Spot Special" cupcake, made with moist cake and creamy frosting in a variety of delicious flavors.
- Experiences: Treat yourself to a sweet indulgence at The Sweet Spot Bakery as you peruse the colorful display of freshly baked goodies. The stall often features seasonal specials and holiday-themed treats, making it a favorite destination for locals and visitors alike.
- Tips on Street Food Safety: While enjoying treats from The Sweet Spot Bakery, be sure to choose items that are packaged and handled with care. Avoid foods that have

been sitting out for long periods and opt for freshly prepared treats. Look for vendors who adhere to proper hygiene practices and ensure that their food is stored and displayed in a clean and sanitary manner.

5. The Pizza Peddlers

- Location: Various locations around Reno (Check their social media for updates)
- Highlights: The Pizza Peddlers are a mobile pizza kitchen on wheels, specializing in artisanal wood-fired pizzas made with fresh, locally sourced ingredients. With their custom-built pizza oven and handcrafted dough, they offer a unique and delicious dining experience.
- Signature Dishes: The Pizza Peddlers offer a variety of gourmet pizzas, including classic Margherita, pepperoni, and specialty options like prosciutto and arugula. Each pizza is hand-tossed and cooked to perfection in their wood-fired oven, resulting in a crispy crust and deliciously melty cheese.
- Experiences: Enjoy the aroma of freshly baked pizza as you watch the Pizza Peddlers work their magic in their mobile kitchen. With their friendly service and customizable menu options, they provide a fun and interactive dining experience that's perfect for gatherings and events.
- Tips on Street Food Safety: While dining at The Pizza Peddlers, ensure that your pizza is cooked thoroughly and served hot. Check that the vendor follows proper food handling and storage practices, and opt for toppings that are fresh and of high quality. Be mindful of any food allergies and inquire about ingredients if needed.

6. Reno's Finest BBQ Pit

- Location: 345 Maple Avenue, Reno, NV 89501
- Highlights: Reno's Finest BBQ Pit is a local favorite for mouthwatering barbecue dishes cooked low and slow over wood-fired pits. Known for their tender meats and flavorful sauces, this food stall is a must-visit for barbecue enthusiasts.
- Signature Dishes: Indulge in a variety of barbecue classics, including pulled pork sandwiches, beef brisket platters, and smoked ribs. Don't miss out on their signature dish, the "Pitmaster's Platter," featuring a generous assortment of meats and sides.
- Experiences: Enjoy the smoky aroma of slow-cooked barbecue as you watch the skilled pitmasters work their magic. With its casual outdoor seating and friendly atmosphere, Reno's Finest BBQ Pit offers a relaxed dining experience that's perfect for meat lovers.
- Tips on Street Food Safety: When dining at Reno's Finest BBQ Pit, ensure that your barbecue is cooked thoroughly and served piping hot. Look for vendors who adhere to proper food safety practices and maintain clean cooking equipment.

7. Sushi on the Go

- Location: Mobile food truck (Check their social media for updates on location)
- Highlights: Sushi on the Go brings the flavors of Japan to the streets of Reno with their fresh and delicious sushi creations. From classic rolls to inventive specialties, this food truck offers a convenient and tasty option for sushi lovers on the move.

- Signature Dishes: Treat yourself to an assortment of sushi rolls, nigiri, and sashimi, made with the freshest seafood and highest quality ingredients. Be sure to try their signature "Reno Roll," featuring local favorites like smoked trout and avocado.
- Experiences: Experience the art of sushi-making up close as you watch the skilled chefs prepare your order on the spot. With its convenient mobile setup and quick service, Sushi on the Go is perfect for a quick and satisfying meal on the run.
- Tips on Street Food Safety: When enjoying sushi from Sushi on the Go, ensure that your seafood is fresh and properly handled. Look for vendors who use high-quality ingredients and maintain clean preparation surfaces.

Tips on Street Food Safety

- Choose reputable vendors: Look for street food stalls with a clean and well-maintained appearance. Vendors who prioritize hygiene are more likely to follow safe food handling practices.
- Opt for freshly prepared food: Choose dishes that are cooked to order and served hot. Avoid foods that have been sitting out for extended periods or appear stale.
- Check food temperatures: Ensure that hot foods are served at the appropriate temperature to prevent the growth of harmful bacteria. Cold foods should be properly chilled to reduce the risk of foodborne illness.
- Wash your hands: Before eating street food, wash your hands thoroughly with soap and water or use hand sanitizer. This helps prevent the spread of germs and reduces the risk of contamination.

- Be mindful of allergies: If you have food allergies or dietary restrictions, be sure to inquire about ingredients and ask the vendor if they can accommodate your needs.
- Trust your instincts: If something seems off or if you're unsure about the cleanliness of a street food stall, it's better to err on the side of caution and choose another vendor.

Exploring Reno's street food scene is a delicious adventure that allows you to sample a diverse array of flavors and culinary creations. With these top recommended street food stalls, you're sure to discover some of the city's most delectable eats while enjoying the vibrant atmosphere of Reno's bustling streets.

CHAPTER 9

Modern Shopping Centers

Experience the convenience and variety of modern shopping experiences in Reno at these contemporary shopping malls and retail complexes. From upscale boutiques to department stores and entertainment venues, these shopping centers offer something for everyone, making them perfect destinations for leisurely shopping outings and entertainment excursions.

1. Meadowood Mall

- Location: 5000 Meadowood Mall Cir, Reno, NV 89502
- Description: Meadowood Mall is Reno's premier shopping destination, featuring over 100 stores, including department stores, specialty retailers, and upscale boutiques. With its modern architecture and spacious layout, Meadowood Mall offers a comfortable and convenient shopping experience for visitors of all ages.
- Retail Offerings: Explore a diverse array of shops and boutiques, including popular brands like Macy's, JCPenney, H&M, and Sephora. From fashion and accessories to electronics, home goods, and more, Meadowood Mall has everything you need for a successful shopping trip.
- Dining Options: Refuel and recharge at Meadowood Mall's food court, which features a variety of dining options ranging from fast-casual favorites to international cuisines. Whether you're craving pizza, sushi, or a hearty sandwich, you'll find plenty of delicious options to satisfy your hunger.

- Entertainment: After a day of shopping, catch a movie at the Century Theatres located within the mall or enjoy some family-friendly fun at the arcade and play area. Meadowood Mall also hosts special events and promotions throughout the year, so be sure to check their website for the latest updates.
- Parking: Meadowood Mall offers ample free parking for shoppers, with both surface lot and garage parking available for added convenience. Handicap-accessible parking spaces are also provided near mall entrances for those with mobility needs.
- Hours: Monday-Saturday: 10:00 AM - 9:00 PM, Sunday: 11:00 AM - 6:00 PM

2. The Summit Reno

- Location: 13925 S Virginia St, Reno, NV 89511
- Description: The Summit Reno is a modern lifestyle center offering a unique shopping and dining experience in a picturesque outdoor setting. With its upscale shops, gourmet restaurants, and entertainment options, The Summit Reno is a favorite destination for locals and visitors alike.
- Retail Offerings: Browse a curated selection of upscale retailers and specialty shops at The Summit Reno, including brands like Apple, lululemon, Pottery Barn, and Williams Sonoma. From fashion and beauty to home decor and electronics, you'll find everything you need for a stylish and sophisticated lifestyle.
- Dining Options: Indulge in gourmet cuisine and casual dining options at The Summit Reno's diverse selection of restaurants and eateries. Whether you're craving sushi,

steak, or artisanal pizza, you'll find plenty of delicious options to tempt your taste buds.

- Entertainment: Catch a movie at the luxury Galaxy Theatres, which offers plush seating, state-of-the-art technology, and a full-service bar for the ultimate movie-watching experience. The Summit Reno also hosts live music performances, outdoor events, and seasonal festivals throughout the year.
- Parking: The Summit Reno offers complimentary parking for shoppers, with both surface lot and garage parking available onsite. Handicap-accessible parking spaces are provided near mall entrances for added convenience.
- Hours: Monday-Saturday: 10:00 AM - 9:00 PM, Sunday: 11:00 AM - 6:00 PM

3. Outlets at Legends Sparks

- Location: 1310 Scheels Dr, Sparks, NV 89434
- Description: The Outlets at Legends Sparks is a premier outlet shopping destination located just a short drive from downtown Reno. Featuring a mix of outlet stores, restaurants, and entertainment options, The Outlets at Legends Sparks offer unbeatable savings on designer brands and everyday essentials.
- Retail Offerings: Shop top brands at discounted prices at The Outlets at Legends Sparks, including Nike, Coach, Levi's, and Gap. Whether you're looking for fashion, footwear, accessories, or home goods, you'll find a wide selection of high-quality products at unbeatable prices.
- Dining Options: Refuel and recharge at The Outlets at Legends Sparks' diverse selection of restaurants and eateries, ranging from casual cafes to family-friendly

favorites. Grab a quick bite to eat or sit down for a leisurely meal before continuing your shopping adventure.

- Entertainment: After a day of shopping, catch a game at the nearby Greater Nevada Field, home to the Reno Aces baseball team and Reno 1868 FC soccer team. The Outlets at Legends Sparks also host special events, live music performances, and seasonal celebrations throughout the year.
- Parking: The Outlets at Legends Sparks offer ample free parking for shoppers, with both surface lot and garage parking available onsite. Handicap-accessible parking spaces are provided near mall entrances for added convenience.
- Hours: Monday-Saturday: 10:00 AM - 9:00 PM, Sunday: 11:00 AM - 6:00 PM

4. Reno Town Mall

- Location: 4001 S Virginia St, Reno, NV 89502
- Description: Reno Town Mall is a modern shopping center conveniently located in the heart of Reno, offering a mix of national retailers, local boutiques, and dining options. With its central location and diverse array of shops, Reno Town Mall is a convenient destination for all your shopping needs.
- Retail Offerings: Explore a variety of shops and stores at Reno Town Mall, including clothing retailers, electronics stores, beauty salons, and more. Whether you're shopping for fashion essentials, tech gadgets, or gifts for loved ones, you'll find plenty of options to choose from.
- Dining Options: Grab a bite to eat at one of Reno Town Mall's casual dining establishments, fast-food eateries, or

coffee shops. From quick and convenient options to sit-down restaurants, there's something to satisfy every craving.

- Entertainment: While Reno Town Mall primarily focuses on shopping and dining, you can also catch a movie at the nearby Century Park Lane 16 movie theater or enjoy a leisurely stroll around the mall's indoor concourse.
- Parking: Reno Town Mall offers ample free parking for shoppers, with both surface lot and garage parking available for added convenience. Handicap-accessible parking spaces are provided near mall entrances for those with mobility needs.
- Hours: Monday-Saturday: 10:00 AM - 9:00 PM, Sunday: 11:00 AM - 6:00 PM

5. Park Lane Mall

- Location: 200 S Virginia St, Reno, NV 89501
- Description: Park Lane Mall is a mixed-use development located in downtown Reno, offering a unique blend of retail, dining, entertainment, and residential spaces. With its modern design and vibrant atmosphere, Park Lane Mall is redefining the shopping experience in the heart of the city.
- Retail Offerings: Explore a diverse selection of shops and stores at Park Lane Mall, ranging from national retailers and flagship stores to locally owned boutiques and specialty shops. Whether you're searching for fashion, home decor, or gourmet food items, you'll find it all at Park Lane Mall.
- Dining Options: Indulge your taste buds at Park Lane Mall's eclectic mix of restaurants, cafes, and eateries,

offering everything from gourmet cuisine to casual fare. Whether you're craving international flavors, comfort food classics, or artisanal delights, there's something to please every palate.

- Entertainment: Park Lane Mall is more than just a shopping destination – it's a vibrant community hub where you can enjoy live music performances, art exhibitions, and special events throughout the year. Check the mall's event calendar for upcoming happenings and activities.
- Parking: Park Lane Mall offers convenient parking options for shoppers, with both surface lot and garage parking available onsite. Handicap-accessible parking spaces are provided near mall entrances for those with mobility needs.
- Hours: Monday-Saturday: 10:00 AM - 9:00 PM, Sunday: 11:00 AM - 6:00 PM

6. Legends at Sparks Marina

- Location: 1310 Scheels Dr, Sparks, NV 89434
- Description: Legends at Sparks Marina is a premier outdoor shopping destination located just minutes from downtown Reno. With its scenic waterfront location and wide range of retail, dining, and entertainment options, Legends offers a unique shopping experience for visitors of all ages.
- Retail Offerings: Shop the latest trends and styles at Legends' diverse selection of retailers, including national chains, specialty stores, and designer boutiques. From fashion and accessories to home decor and electronics, you'll find everything you need for a day of retail therapy.
- Dining Options: Indulge in a culinary adventure at Legends' array of restaurants, cafes, and eateries, offering everything from casual dining options to upscale cuisine.

Whether you're in the mood for sushi, burgers, or gourmet pizza, there's a restaurant to satisfy every craving.

- Entertainment: After a day of shopping and dining, relax and unwind at Legends' outdoor amphitheater, where you can enjoy live music performances, outdoor movies, and community events. The marina also offers opportunities for boating, fishing, and water sports, making it a popular destination for outdoor enthusiasts.

- Parking: Legends at Sparks Marina offers ample free parking for shoppers, with both surface lot and garage parking available onsite. Handicap-accessible parking spaces are provided near mall entrances for those with mobility needs.

- Hours: Monday-Saturday: 10:00 AM - 9:00 PM, Sunday: 11:00 AM - 6:00 PM

Explore Reno's modern shopping centers and discover a world of retail, dining, and entertainment options waiting to be explored. Whether you're searching for the latest fashion trends, unique gifts, or delicious cuisine, these shopping destinations offer something for everyone, making them perfect destinations for a day of leisurely exploration and enjoyment.

Local Markets

Explore the vibrant and bustling markets of Reno, where you can immerse yourself in the city's vibrant culture, sample delicious local delicacies, and discover unique handmade crafts and souvenirs. From fresh produce to artisanal goods, these markets offer a diverse array of treasures waiting to be explored.

1. Riverside Farmers Market

- Location: Riverside Drive, Reno, NV 89503

- Operating Hours: Saturdays, 9:00 AM - 1:00 PM (May through October)
- Specialties: The Riverside Farmers Market is a vibrant outdoor market featuring a wide selection of locally grown produce, fresh flowers, artisanal foods, and handmade crafts. From farm-fresh fruits and vegetables to homemade jams and baked goods, you'll find a variety of treats to tantalize your taste buds.
- Cultural Significance: The Riverside Farmers Market is a beloved community gathering place where locals and visitors alike come together to support local farmers and artisans. The market showcases the rich agricultural heritage of the region and promotes sustainable farming practices.
- Tips: Don't be afraid to haggle with vendors for the best prices on fresh produce and artisanal goods. Be sure to arrive early to beat the crowds and snag the freshest produce and most coveted items.

2. Reno Street Market

- Location: Downtown Reno, NV 89501
- Operating Hours: Sundays, 10:00 AM - 4:00 PM
- Specialties: The Reno Street Market is a bustling open-air market featuring a diverse array of vendors selling everything from handmade jewelry and clothing to vintage treasures and antiques. You'll also find a variety of food trucks offering delicious snacks and refreshments.
- Cultural Significance: The Reno Street Market is a vibrant hub of creativity and entrepreneurship, showcasing the talents of local artisans and small businesses. The market's

eclectic mix of vendors reflects the diverse and dynamic spirit of Reno's downtown community.

- Tips: Take your time exploring the market's winding aisles and hidden corners to discover unique treasures and one-of-a-kind finds. Be sure to bring cash as some vendors may not accept credit cards.

3. Great Basin Community Food Co-op

- Location: 240 Court St, Reno, NV 89501
- Operating Hours: Monday-Saturday, 9:00 AM - 8:00 PM; Sunday, 10:00 AM - 6:00 PM
- Specialties: The Great Basin Community Food Co-op is a local grocery store and market specializing in organic and locally sourced products. Here, you'll find a wide selection of fresh produce, bulk goods, artisanal cheeses, and specialty items from local producers.
- Cultural Significance: The Great Basin Community Food Co-op is more than just a market – it's a community hub where like-minded individuals come together to support sustainable agriculture and healthy living. The co-op hosts events, workshops, and educational programs aimed at promoting environmental stewardship and food justice.
- Tips: Take advantage of the co-op's bulk section to stock up on pantry staples like grains, nuts, and spices. Don't miss the deli counter, where you can grab a freshly made sandwich or salad for a quick and delicious lunch.

4. Midtown Farmers Market

- Location: 777 S Center St, Reno, NV 89501
- Operating Hours: Saturdays, 9:00 AM - 1:00 PM (June through September)

- Specialties: The Midtown Farmers Market is a vibrant neighborhood market featuring a diverse array of local vendors, artisans, and food trucks. Here, you'll find farm-fresh produce, handmade crafts, artisanal foods, and live music performances.
- Cultural Significance: The Midtown Farmers Market celebrates the vibrant culture and creativity of Reno's Midtown district, showcasing the talents of local artists, musicians, and small businesses. The market's relaxed and friendly atmosphere makes it a favorite destination for families and community members of all ages.
- Tips: Arrive early to enjoy the best selection of produce and artisanal goods. Be sure to grab a bite to eat from one of the food trucks and enjoy a leisurely stroll through the market while taking in the sights and sounds of Reno's vibrant Midtown neighborhood.

Explore Reno's local markets and discover the rich tapestry of flavors, sights, and sounds that make up the city's vibrant culinary and cultural landscape. Whether you're searching for fresh produce, unique artisanal goods, or simply looking to soak up the atmosphere, these markets offer an authentic and unforgettable shopping experience.

Boutiques

Indulge in a boutique shopping experience in Reno, where you'll find an array of chic and stylish shops offering curated selections of fashion, accessories, and home decor. From trendy clothing boutiques to charming gift shops, these establishments cater to fashion-forward individuals seeking unique and stylish finds. Explore the following boutiques to discover the latest trends, timeless classics, and one-of-a-kind pieces that will elevate your wardrobe and home décor.

1. Pantry Products

- Location: 20 St Lawrence Ave, Reno, NV 89509
- Description: Pantry Products is a charming boutique specializing in handcrafted bath and body products made with natural and locally sourced ingredients. From artisanal soaps and bath bombs to luxurious body scrubs and skincare essentials, Pantry Products offers a wide range of products to pamper yourself or treat someone special.
- Specialties: The boutique's signature products include their handmade soaps, which come in a variety of delightful scents and are perfect for indulgent self-care rituals. Pantry Products also offers DIY workshops where you can learn to make your own bath and body products using natural ingredients.
- Ambiance: Step into Pantry Products and immerse yourself in a cozy and inviting atmosphere filled with the soothing scents of essential oils and botanicals. The boutique's rustic decor and friendly staff create a welcoming environment where you can relax and explore their selection of handcrafted treasures.

2. NeverEnder

- Location: 857 S Virginia St, Reno, NV 89501
- Description: NeverEnder is a trendy boutique located in Reno's Midtown district, offering a curated selection of clothing, accessories, and home goods for the modern bohemian. From flowy dresses and embroidered tops to statement jewelry and eclectic home decor, NeverEnder

specializes in unique and stylish pieces that reflect the free-spirited vibe of its customers.

- Specialties: The boutique's bohemian-inspired clothing and accessories are perfect for fashion-forward individuals looking to express their individuality and creativity. Whether you're searching for the perfect festival outfit or a unique piece to add to your everyday wardrobe, NeverEnder has something for everyone.
- Ambiance: Step into NeverEnder and discover a laid-back and eclectic atmosphere filled with colorful textiles, vintage-inspired furnishings, and bohemian accents. The boutique's friendly staff are always on hand to offer styling tips and recommendations, creating a personalized shopping experience for every customer.

3. Sierra Belle Boutique

- Location: 726 S Virginia St, Reno, NV 89501
- Description: Sierra Belle Boutique is a stylish women's clothing boutique located in the heart of downtown Reno. With its curated selection of trendy apparel, accessories, and footwear, Sierra Belle offers fashion-forward women the latest styles and trends at affordable prices.
- Specialties: The boutique's signature pieces include on-trend clothing and accessories that are perfect for both casual and dressy occasions. From chic dresses and cozy sweaters to statement jewelry and stylish handbags, Sierra Belle has everything you need to elevate your wardrobe.
- Ambiance: Step into Sierra Belle Boutique and experience a modern and inviting atmosphere filled with racks of stylish clothing and accessories. The boutique's bright and airy space is perfect for leisurely browsing and trying on

your favorite finds, while the knowledgeable staff are always available to offer fashion advice and assistance.

4. The Niche

- Location: 1175 W Moana Ln, Reno, NV 89509
- Description: The Niche is a charming boutique specializing in unique gifts, home decor, and accessories. Located in the Plumgate Shopping Center, The Niche offers a carefully curated selection of items sourced from local artisans, independent designers, and fair trade suppliers.
- Specialties: The boutique's eclectic mix of products includes handmade jewelry, artisanal candles, whimsical home decor, and much more. Whether you're shopping for a special occasion or simply treating yourself, The Niche has a wide range of treasures waiting to be discovered.
- Ambiance: Step into The Niche and discover a warm and welcoming environment filled with delightful surprises at every turn. The boutique's cozy layout and friendly staff create a relaxed shopping experience where you can take your time exploring their selection of unique gifts and accessories.

Explore Reno's boutiques and uncover a world of style, creativity, and individuality. Whether you're searching for the perfect outfit, a unique accessory, or a thoughtful gift, these shops offer an unparalleled shopping experience that celebrates personal style and expression.

Souvenir Shopping Guide

When visiting Reno, you'll undoubtedly want to take home a piece of the city's vibrant culture and unique charm. From locally crafted goods to iconic symbols of the area, there are plenty of authentic souvenirs to choose from that capture the spirit of Reno. To ensure your memento is truly memorable, consider the following recommendations for authentic local items:

1. Artisanal Pottery

- Description: Reno is home to a thriving community of talented ceramic artists who create stunning pottery pieces inspired by the region's natural beauty and cultural heritage. Look for handcrafted mugs, bowls, and vases adorned with intricate designs and vibrant glazes that reflect the colors of the Nevada landscape.
- Where to Find: Visit local art galleries, pottery studios, and artisan markets to discover one-of-a-kind pottery pieces crafted by Reno's talented artisans. Look for pieces that showcase the artist's unique style and incorporate elements of Reno's scenery, such as desert motifs or mountain landscapes.
- Why Choose: Artisanal pottery not only serves as a beautiful and functional souvenir but also allows you to support local artists and artisans. Each piece is a unique work of art that captures the essence of Reno's artistic community and adds a touch of handmade charm to your home.

2. Handmade Jewelry

Description: Reno's vibrant arts scene extends to jewelry design, with local artisans creating stunning pieces inspired by the city's natural surroundings and cultural influences. Look for handmade necklaces, bracelets, and earrings crafted from locally sourced materials such as gemstones, metals, and beads.

- Where to Find: Explore local boutiques, artisan markets, and craft fairs to discover a wide range of handmade jewelry designs crafted by Reno's talented artisans. Look for pieces that showcase unique craftsmanship and incorporate elements of Reno's landscape or heritage.
- Why Choose: Handmade jewelry offers a personal and meaningful souvenir that reflects Reno's artistic spirit and creativity. Whether you opt for a delicate necklace adorned with a sparkling gemstone or a bold statement piece inspired by the city's rugged terrain, you'll treasure your Reno-made jewelry for years to come.

3. Native American Art

- Description: Reno is situated in close proximity to several Native American reservations, making it an ideal destination to explore Indigenous art and culture. Look for authentic Native American artwork, including pottery, textiles, beadwork, and traditional crafts, that celebrates the rich heritage of the region's Indigenous peoples.
- Where to Find: Visit local galleries, museums, and cultural centers that showcase Native American art and artifacts. Look for pieces created by local Indigenous artists and artisans, as well as authentic crafts sourced directly from tribal communities in the region.

Why Choose: Native American art serves as a powerful and meaningful souvenir that honors the cultural heritage of the region's Indigenous peoples. By supporting Indigenous artists and artisans, you can help preserve traditional craftsmanship and contribute to the continued vitality of Native American culture in Reno and beyond.

4. Local Food and Beverages

- Description: Reno boasts a vibrant culinary scene that reflects the region's diverse cultural influences and agricultural abundance. Look for locally made food and beverage products, such as artisanal chocolates, gourmet jams, craft beers, and locally roasted coffee, that showcase the flavors and ingredients of the area.
- Where to Find: Explore local farmers' markets, specialty food stores, and gourmet shops to discover a wide range of locally made food and beverage products. Look for items that highlight the unique flavors and culinary traditions of Reno and the surrounding region.
- Why Choose: Local food and beverages offer a delicious and memorable way to experience the flavors of Reno. Whether you're indulging in a box of handmade chocolates or sipping on a locally brewed beer, you'll savor the taste of the region long after your visit has ended.

5. Vintage Postcards and Memorabilia

- Description: Vintage postcards and memorabilia offer a nostalgic glimpse into Reno's storied past and colorful history. Look for antique postcards, retro travel posters, and vintage souvenirs that capture iconic landmarks, historic events, and bygone eras of the city.
- Where to Find: Browse antique shops, vintage stores, and collectibles markets to discover a treasure trove of vintage postcards and memorabilia celebrating Reno's history. Look for items that evoke a sense of nostalgia and offer a glimpse into the city's past.
- Why Choose: Vintage postcards and memorabilia serve as charming and nostalgic souvenirs that celebrate Reno's rich

history and heritage. Whether you're collecting postcards featuring classic Reno landmarks or vintage travel posters depicting the city's golden age, you'll enjoy reminiscing about your time in Reno for years to come.

Tips for Choosing Memorable Souvenirs:

- Authenticity: Look for souvenirs that are authentically made or sourced from local artisans, craftsmen, and Indigenous communities in the Reno area.
- Quality: Choose souvenirs that are well-crafted and made from high-quality materials, ensuring they will last for years to come and serve as cherished mementos of your visit.
- Meaningful Connection: Select souvenirs that resonate with you personally and evoke fond memories of your time in Reno, whether it's a piece of artwork, a handmade craft, or a delicious local treat.
- Support Local: By purchasing souvenirs from local artisans, businesses, and Indigenous communities, you can support the local economy and contribute to the cultural vitality of Reno.

Choose souvenirs that capture the spirit of Reno and serve as lasting reminders of your unforgettable journey in the "Biggest Little City in the World." Whether you opt for handmade pottery, locally made jewelry, or vintage memorabilia, your chosen memento will help keep the memories of your Reno adventure alive for years to come.

CHAPTER 10

CULTURAL EXPERIENCES

Festivals and Events

Experience the vibrant culture and lively atmosphere of Reno through its diverse array of festivals, events, and cultural celebrations. From music concerts and art exhibitions to food fairs and outdoor extravaganzas, there's always something exciting happening in the city. Explore the following festivals and events to immerse yourself in the local culture and create unforgettable memories during your visit to Reno:

1. Reno River Festival

- Description: The Reno River Festival is a premier outdoor event that celebrates the city's vibrant riverfront and adventurous spirit. Held annually along the Truckee River in downtown Reno, this festival features thrilling whitewater competitions, kayaking demonstrations, live music performances, and family-friendly activities.
- Significance: The Reno River Festival showcases Reno's love for outdoor recreation and highlights the importance of the Truckee River as a recreational and ecological resource for the community. It also promotes environmental stewardship and water conservation efforts.
- Activities: Attendees can watch professional kayakers navigate through challenging whitewater courses, participate in rafting and tubing excursions, explore vendor booths offering outdoor gear and apparel, and enjoy live music concerts and food vendors along the riverfront.
- Event Dates: Typically held in May each year.

- Location: Downtown Reno along the Truckee River.
- Admission: Free to attend; some activities may require a fee.

2. Artown

- Description: Artown is Reno's month-long summer arts festival, showcasing a diverse range of cultural performances, visual arts exhibitions, workshops, and community events throughout the city. From music and dance to theater and film, Artown offers something for everyone to enjoy.
- Significance: Artown aims to enrich the cultural vitality of Reno by providing accessible and inclusive arts experiences for residents and visitors alike. The festival celebrates creativity, diversity, and artistic expression, showcasing the talents of local and international artists.
- Activities: Attendees can attend live music concerts, dance performances, art exhibitions, theater productions, film screenings, and interactive workshops held at various venues across Reno. Special events such as the Artown Opening Night Jubilee and closing fireworks display add to the festival's excitement.
- Event Dates: July 1st - July 31st (annually).
- Location: Various venues throughout Reno.
- Admission: Many events are free; some may require tickets or registration.

3. Great Reno Balloon Race

- Description: The Great Reno Balloon Race is the largest free hot-air balloon event in the world, attracting thousands of spectators each year to witness the spectacle of colorful balloons filling the sky. Held at Rancho San Rafael Regional Park, this three-day event features dawn balloon launches, balloon glow events, and family-friendly activities.

- Significance: The Great Reno Balloon Race has become a beloved tradition in the community, symbolizing Reno's spirit of adventure and love for outdoor recreation. It also serves as a platform for balloon enthusiasts and pilots from around the world to showcase their skills and creativity.
- Activities: Visitors can watch as dozens of hot-air balloons take flight at sunrise, participate in balloon rides (by reservation), enjoy live music performances, food vendors, and children's activities at the Balloon Boulevard, and witness the breathtaking spectacle of the "Super Glow" evening events.
- Event Dates: Typically held in early September each year.
- Location: Rancho San Rafael Regional Park, Reno.
- Admission: Free to attend; some activities may require a fee.

4. Street Vibrations Motorcycle Festival

- Description: The Street Vibrations Motorcycle Festival is a high-energy event that celebrates motorcycle culture and lifestyle in Reno and the surrounding region. Spanning several days, this festival features live music performances, motorcycle stunt shows, bike rallies, poker runs, and a vendor expo showcasing the latest motorcycle gear and accessories.
- Significance: Street Vibrations brings together motorcycle enthusiasts from all walks of life to celebrate their passion for two-wheeled machines and the open road. It promotes

camaraderie, friendship, and a sense of community among riders and fans alike.

- Activities: Attendees can enjoy live music concerts featuring local and national bands, marvel at thrilling motorcycle stunt performances, participate in bike parades and group rides, and explore the vendor village offering a wide range of motorcycle-related products and services.
- Event Dates: Typically held in late September each year.
- Location: Various venues throughout Reno, including downtown streets and casinos.
- Admission: Free to attend; some activities may require a fee.

5. Reno Jazz Festival

- Description: The Reno Jazz Festival is a multi-day celebration of jazz music featuring performances by world-class musicians, student ensembles, and emerging artists. Hosted by the University of Nevada, Reno, this annual event includes concerts, workshops, competitions, and jam sessions held at various venues across the city.
- Significance: The Reno Jazz Festival promotes jazz education and appreciation while providing a platform for young musicians to showcase their talents and learn from seasoned professionals. It attracts jazz enthusiasts from around the world and fosters a vibrant jazz community in Reno.
- Activities: Attendees can enjoy performances by renowned jazz artists and student bands, participate in workshops and masterclasses covering a range of topics related to jazz

music and improvisation, and explore the vendor booths offering jazz-related merchandise and instruments.

- Event Dates: Typically held in April each year.
- Location: Various venues on the University of Nevada, Reno campus and downtown Reno.
- Admission: Some events may require tickets or registration; check the festival website for details.

6. Hot August Nights

- Description: Hot August Nights is a nostalgic celebration of classic cars, music, and Americana culture that takes place in Reno and surrounding areas. This multi-day event features car shows, cruises, live entertainment, and retro-themed activities that transport attendees back to the heyday of the 1950s and '60s.
- Significance: Hot August Nights celebrates Reno's automotive heritage and love for vintage cars while providing a fun and nostalgic experience for attendees of all ages. It attracts car enthusiasts, music lovers, and families looking to relive the golden era of American motoring.
- Activities: Attendees can admire thousands of classic cars on display at various locations throughout Reno, participate in car cruises and parades, enjoy live music performances featuring tribute bands and '50s and '60s artists, and shop for vintage memorabilia and retro-themed merchandise.
- Event Dates: Typically held in early August each year.
- Location: Various venues throughout Reno, including downtown streets and casinos.
- Admission: Some events may require tickets or registration; check the event website for details.

7. Reno Rodeo

- Description: The Reno Rodeo is one of the largest and most prestigious rodeo events in the country, attracting professional cowboys and cowgirls from around the world to compete in various rodeo events such as bull riding, barrel racing, steer wrestling, and more. In addition to the rodeo competitions, the event features a carnival, live entertainment, and western-themed activities.
- Significance: The Reno Rodeo celebrates Nevada's cowboy heritage and western culture while providing thrilling entertainment for rodeo fans and spectators. It showcases the skills and athleticism of rodeo athletes and promotes the values of sportsmanship, tradition, and community spirit.
- Activities: Attendees can watch adrenaline-pumping rodeo competitions, enjoy live music performances, explore the carnival rides and games, participate in western-themed activities such as cowboy poetry readings and western art exhibits, and shop for cowboy boots, hats, and other western gear.
- Event Dates: Typically held in June each year.
- Location: Reno-Sparks Livestock Events Center, Reno.
- Admission: Tickets required for rodeo events and some activities; check the event website for details.

Practical Information:

- Plan your visit to coincide with the festival or event of your choice.
- Check the official websites or event organizers for the most up-to-date information on dates, locations, and activities.

- Arrive early for popular events to secure parking and get the best viewing spots.
- Dress appropriately for outdoor events and bring sunscreen, water, and snacks.
- Be respectful of local customs and traditions, and follow any rules or guidelines provided by event organizers.

Immerse yourself in the vibrant atmosphere and rich cultural experiences of Reno's festivals and events, and create unforgettable memories during your visit to the city. Whether you're a music enthusiast, car aficionado, or rodeo fan, there's something for everyone to enjoy at Reno's diverse array of festivals and celebrations throughout the year.

Arts Galleries

Discover the vibrant art scene of Reno through its eclectic array of galleries showcasing local and international talent. From contemporary works to traditional masterpieces, these galleries offer a diverse range of artistic expressions and styles. Immerse yourself in the creative energy of the city and explore the following must-visit arts galleries:

1. Sierra Arts Gallery

- Descriptio: Sierra Arts Gallery is a nonprofit organization dedicated to supporting and promoting local artists and arts education inn the Reno-Tahoe region. The gallery showcases a rotating selection of contemporary artwork across various mediums, including painting, sculpture, photography, and mixed media.
- Exhibits: Explore curated exhibitions featuring emerging and established artists from the local community, as well as

guest artists from around the world. The gallery also hosts artist talks, receptions, and workshops to engage with the public and foster artistic dialogue.

- Location: 17 S Virginia St, Reno, NV.
- Hours: Open Tuesday-Saturday; hours vary.
- Admission: Free admission; donations appreciated.

2. Stremmel Gallery

- Description: Stremmel Gallery is a premier art gallery in Reno specializing in contemporary and modern art by renowned artists from the United States and abroad. With a focus on painting, sculpture, and works on paper, the gallery presents a curated selection of museum-quality artwork in a sophisticated setting.
- Exhibits: Experience thought-provoking exhibitions featuring works by contemporary artists pushing the boundaries of artistic expression. From abstract compositions to figurative realism, the gallery showcases a diverse range of styles and techniques.
- Location: 1400 S Virginia St, Reno, NV.
- Hours: Open Tuesday-Saturday; hours vary.
- Admission: Free admission; artworks available for purchase.

3. Nevada Fine Arts

- Description: Nevada Fine Arts is a comprehensive art supply store and gallery that has been serving the creative community of Reno for over 50 years. In addition to offering a wide range of art supplies and materials, the gallery features rotating exhibitions of local artists' work in various mediums.

- Exhibits: Browse through the gallery's diverse collection of paintings, drawings, ceramics, and mixed media artworks created by talented artists from the region. The gallery also hosts art classes, workshops, and events for artists of all skill levels.
- Location: 1301 S Virginia St, Reno, NV.
- Hours: Open Monday-Saturday; hours vary.
- Admission: Free admission; artworks available for purchase.

4. Liberty Fine Art Gallery

- Description: Liberty Fine Art Gallery is a contemporary art gallery located in the heart of downtown Reno, showcasing a curated selection of original artworks by local and regional artists. The gallery features paintings, sculptures, glass art, and jewelry in a range of styles and aesthetics.
- Exhibits: Discover unique and captivating artworks that reflect the beauty and diversity of the Reno-Tahoe region. From landscapes inspired by the Sierra Nevada mountains to abstract compositions exploring color and form, the gallery offers something for every art enthusiast.
- Location: 100 W Liberty St, Reno, NV.
- Hours: Open Tuesday-Saturday; hours vary.
- Admission: Free admission; artworks available for purchase.

Practical Information:

- Check the gallery websites or contact them directly for information on current exhibitions, artists, and events.
- Support local artists by purchasing artwork directly from galleries or attending art shows and exhibitions.

- Consider joining gallery memberships or mailing lists to stay informed about upcoming exhibitions and special promotions.
- Respect the artwork and gallery space by refraining from touching the artwork and following any gallery guidelines or rules.

Immerse yourself in Reno's vibrant arts scene by visiting its top galleries showcasing the talent and creativity of local and regional artists. From contemporary masterpieces to traditional classics, these galleries offer a diverse range of artistic experiences for visitors to explore and enjoy.

Local Customs and Etiquette

When visiting Reno, understanding and respecting local customs and cultural etiquette can significantly enhance your experience and interactions with the locals. Reno is a city rich in diversity and community spirit, blending the relaxed ambiance of the West with the vibrancy of a growing urban center. Here's an in-depth guide to navigating the cultural landscape of Reno with respect and appreciation.

Understanding Reno's Cultural Landscape

Friendly and Inclusive Attitude

- Renoites, as the locals are known, are generally friendly and inclusive. The city's atmosphere reflects a mix of small-town charm and big-city vibrancy, with a welcoming attitude towards visitors. You'll often find locals ready to offer directions, recommend their favorite spots, or share stories about the city.

Outdoor Lifestyle

- Reno's proximity to the Sierra Nevada mountains, Lake Tahoe, and numerous parks makes outdoor activities a cornerstone of the local lifestyle. Hiking, skiing, biking, and fishing are popular pastimes, and participating in these activities is a great way to connect with the community.

Embracing Diversity

- Reno is a melting pot of cultures, with a growing population that includes people from various ethnic backgrounds and lifestyles. The city celebrates this diversity through cultural festivals, events, and a wide range of culinary offerings. Being open-minded and respectful of different cultures is highly valued.

Social Etiquette

Greetings and Introductions

- Handshake and Smiles: A firm handshake and a friendly smile are standard greetings in Reno. When meeting someone for the first time, it's polite to shake hands and make eye contact. Among friends and family, hugs are also common.
- Names and Titles: Using titles and last names initially, especially in formal settings, is considered respectful until you are invited to use first names. For instance, addressing someone as Mr., Mrs., or Dr. followed by their last name is a safe approach.
- Small Talk: Engage in light conversation topics such as the weather, local events, and outdoor activities. Avoid controversial subjects like politics and religion unless you know the person well.

Conversation Norms

- Active Listening: Show genuine interest in conversations by actively listening and asking follow-up questions. Renoites appreciate when others show curiosity about their city and lifestyle.
- Respect Personal Space: While Renoites are friendly, they also value personal space. Maintain a comfortable distance during conversations, especially with strangers.

Dining Etiquette

- Restaurant Culture: Reno boasts a variety of dining options, from casual eateries to fine dining establishments. It's customary to wait to be seated at restaurants, and making reservations for popular spots is advisable.
- Tipping: Tipping is customary in Reno. A standard tip is 15-20% of the bill in restaurants. For other services like taxis, hairdressers, and hotel staff, a tip of 10-15% is appreciated.
- Local Cuisine: Embrace local dishes and be open to trying new foods. Asking servers for recommendations is a great way to discover Reno's culinary delights.

Dress Code

Casual and Practical Attire

- Reno's dress code is generally casual and practical, reflecting the city's outdoor lifestyle. Jeans, t-shirts, and comfortable shoes are common, especially for daytime activities. When engaging in outdoor sports, appropriate gear such as hiking boots or ski attire is essential.

Dressing Up

- For evening outings, upscale dining, or attending cultural events, smart-casual or business-casual attire is suitable. Women may opt for dresses or nice tops with slacks, while men might choose collared shirts and dress pants. Formal attire is rarely required but appreciated at high-end venues.

Community Engagement

Supporting Local Businesses

- Renoites take pride in their local businesses, from family-owned restaurants to artisanal shops. Supporting local businesses is a way to contribute to the community and experience the unique offerings of the city.

Volunteering and Participation

- Volunteering and participating in community events are valued activities. Whether it's helping out at a local charity, joining a neighborhood cleanup, or attending city council meetings, getting involved shows respect for the community and a commitment to its well-being.

Festivals and Events

Celebrating Local Festivals

- Reno hosts a variety of festivals and events throughout the year, celebrating everything from arts and music to food and culture. Participating in these events is a great way to immerse yourself in the local culture. Some popular festivals include the Reno River Festival, Hot August Nights, and the Great Reno Balloon Race.

Event Etiquette

- Respecting Traditions: When attending cultural events or festivals, show respect for local traditions and customs. Observe how locals participate and follow suit.
- Punctuality: Being on time for events and gatherings is appreciated. If attending a show or performance, arrive early to find your seat and avoid disruptions.

Environmental Awareness

Sustainability Efforts

- Reno places a strong emphasis on sustainability and environmental conservation. Many locals engage in recycling, composting, and reducing waste. Being mindful of your environmental impact, such as using reusable bags and water bottles, aligns with local values.

Respecting Nature

- When exploring Reno's natural attractions, practice Leave No Trace principles. This includes packing out all trash, staying on designated trails, and respecting wildlife. By preserving the natural environment, you contribute to the community's commitment to sustainability.

Practical Tips

Navigating the City

- Public Transportation: Reno's public transportation system, RTC Ride, offers bus services throughout the city. Familiarize yourself with bus routes and schedules for convenient travel.
- Parking: Parking is generally accessible, but be mindful of metered spots and residential parking restrictions.

Downtown areas may have parking garages or paid parking lots.

Safety and Health

- Emergency Services: Dial 911 for emergencies. Familiarize yourself with the locations of nearby hospitals and clinics.
- Weather Preparedness: Reno experiences a high desert climate with hot summers and cold winters. Dress appropriately for the weather, and stay hydrated, especially during outdoor activities.

Additional Cultural Insights

Respect for History and Heritage

- Reno has a rich history, from its indigenous roots to its role in the silver rush and as a gateway to the West. Showing respect for this history, whether by visiting museums, attending historical tours, or simply acknowledging it in conversations, is appreciated by locals.

Art and Music Scene

- Reno has a thriving art and music scene, with numerous galleries, live music venues, and public art installations. Participating in or showing appreciation for these cultural expressions, whether by attending events or purchasing local art, supports the community and its creative endeavors.

Outdoor Recreation Etiquette

- Given Reno's emphasis on outdoor activities, respecting the environment and other outdoor enthusiasts is crucial. This includes following trail etiquette, such as yielding to uphill hikers, not disturbing wildlife, and adhering to posted guidelines in natural areas.

Local Phrases and Expressions

- While not unique to Reno, understanding some common regional phrases can enhance your interactions. Phrases like "Howdy" for a friendly greeting or "Ya'll" when addressing a group can make you feel more integrated into the local culture.

Understanding and embracing Reno's local customs and cultural etiquette not only enhances your travel experience but also fosters positive interactions with the community. By respecting the local culture and participating in the city's vibrant activities, you'll create lasting memories and gain a deeper appreciation for Reno's unique charm.

CHAPTER 11

PRACTICAL INFORMATION

Tourist Information Centers

Tourist information centers play a crucial role in helping visitors navigate a new destination, providing valuable resources, recommendations, and assistance to ensure a smooth and enjoyable travel experience. In Reno, these centers are strategically located to offer convenience and comprehensive information about the city's attractions, accommodations, events, and services. Here's a detailed guide to the main tourist information centers in Reno, highlighting their locations, services, and what visitors can expect.

1. Reno-Tahoe Visitor Information Center

Location

- Address: 1350 Scheels Drive, Suite 250, Sparks, NV 89434
- Phone: +1 775-827-7600
- Website: visitrenotahoe.com

Description

- The Reno-Tahoe Visitor Information Center is one of the most prominent and comprehensive information hubs for travelers in the Reno area. Located in Sparks, just a short drive from downtown Reno, this center serves as an excellent starting point for visitors looking to explore the region.

Services

- Maps and Brochures: A wide array of maps, brochures, and guidebooks are available to help you plan your itinerary.
- Personalized Recommendations: Knowledgeable staff provide personalized recommendations based on your interests, whether it's outdoor activities, dining, or cultural attractions.
- Event Information: Up-to-date information on local events, festivals, and entertainment options.
- Accommodations Assistance: Guidance on finding accommodations to suit your budget and preferences.
- Transportation Information: Details on public transportation, car rentals, and parking in the area.
- Merchandise: A selection of souvenirs and local products for purchase.

Highlights

- Proximity to Shopping and Dining: Located within the Legends Outlets shopping center, visitors can combine their trip to the information center with some shopping and dining.
- Ample Parking: Free parking is available, making it convenient for travelers with vehicles.

2. Downtown Reno Visitor Center

Location

- Address: 135 N Sierra St, Reno, NV 89501
- Phone: +1 775-334-INFO (4636)
- Website: downtownreno.org

Description

- Situated in the heart of Reno, the Downtown Reno Visitor Center is perfect for those staying or starting their journey in the downtown area. This center is easily accessible and close to many of Reno's major hotels, casinos, and attractions.

Services

- Tourist Information: Comprehensive details about local attractions, dining, nightlife, and shopping.
- Event Tickets: Assistance with purchasing tickets for local shows, concerts, and sporting events.
- Walking Tours: Information on self-guided walking tours and organized group tours of downtown Reno.
- Public Transportation: Guidance on navigating the city's bus system and other transportation options.
- Multilingual Support: Assistance available in multiple languages for international visitors.

Highlights

- Central Location: Ideal for visitors staying downtown or planning to explore the urban core.
- Accessibility: Easy access for pedestrians, with nearby public transportation options.
- Local Insights: Staff provide insider tips on the best local spots, hidden gems, and unique experiences.

3. Reno-Sparks Convention Center Information Desk

Location

- Address: 4590 S Virginia St, Reno, NV 89502
- Phone: +1 775-827-7600

- Website: renosparksconventioncenter.com

Description

- The Reno-Sparks Convention Center is a hub for conferences, trade shows, and large events. Its information desk serves attendees and visitors, offering a range of services to enhance their stay in Reno.

Services

- Event Information: Details about current and upcoming events at the convention center.
- Local Attractions: Information on nearby attractions, dining, and entertainment options.
- Transportation: Assistance with transportation needs, including shuttle services, taxis, and public transit.
- Business Services: Access to business amenities such as printing, copying, and Wi-Fi.
- Accommodation Assistance: Help with finding nearby hotels and lodging options.

Highlights

- Event Focused: Ideal for visitors attending events at the convention center.
- Comprehensive Services: Provides a full suite of services tailored to the needs of convention attendees.
- Proximity to Hotels: Close to several major hotels, making it convenient for out-of-town visitors.

4. Greater Reno Chamber of Commerce Visitor Center

Location

- Address: 449 South Virginia St, Reno, NV 89501
- Phone: +1 775-337-3030
- Website: renochamber.org

Description

- The Greater Reno Chamber of Commerce operates a visitor center that serves as a valuable resource for both tourists and business travelers. Located centrally, it's an excellent place to gather information about the city and its offerings.

Services

- Business Resources: Information for business travelers, including networking opportunities and business events.
- Tourist Guides: Access to maps, brochures, and visitor guides.
- Local Recommendations: Expert advice on the best places to eat, stay, and play in Reno.
- Relocation Information: Resources for those considering moving to Reno, including housing and employment information.
- Community Events: Details about local community events and activities.

Highlights

- Business and Leisure: Catered to both tourists and business travelers, offering a unique blend of services.
- Networking Opportunities: Connect with local businesses and professionals.
- Community Focus: Provides insights into the local community and culture.

Practical Tips for Visiting Tourist Information Centers

1. Plan Ahead

- Before visiting, consider making a list of questions or information you need. This will help you make the most of your time at the information center.

2. Be Open to Recommendations

- Staff at these centers are locals with a wealth of knowledge. Be open to their suggestions, which can often lead to discovering hidden gems and unique experiences.

3. Collect Brochures and Maps

- Even in the digital age, having physical maps and brochures can be incredibly handy, especially in areas with limited cell service.

4. Ask About Discounts and Deals

- Information centers often have access to exclusive discounts and deals on attractions, tours, and events. Don't hesitate to ask about any available offers.

5. Respect Local Customs

- When interacting with staff and locals, be polite and respectful. Showing appreciation for their help goes a long way.

By utilizing the services and resources provided by Reno's tourist information centers, you can ensure a well-planned and enjoyable visit, gaining valuable insights and making the most of your time in this vibrant city.

Safety and Security Tips

When visiting Reno, ensuring your safety and security is paramount to enjoying a stress-free and memorable experience. Here are practical tips and precautions to help you stay safe during your trip, along with important emergency information and advice on avoiding common hazards and scams.

General Safety Tips

Stay Aware of Your Surroundings

- Be Vigilant: Always be aware of your surroundings, especially in crowded places, tourist hotspots, and unfamiliar areas.
- Trust Your Instincts: If something feels off or unsafe, trust your instincts and remove yourself from the situation.

Keep Valuables Secure

- Use Hotel Safes: Store valuables such as passports, extra cash, and electronics in the hotel safe.
- Avoid Flashing Wealth: Don't openly display expensive items like jewelry, cameras, or large amounts of cash.
- Secure Your Bags: Use anti-theft bags and keep them close to your body, especially in busy areas.

Use Reputable Transportation Services

- Official Taxis and Rideshares: Use registered taxis or reputable rideshare services like Uber or Lyft. Avoid unlicensed cabs.
- Public Transport: Familiarize yourself with public transportation routes and schedules to avoid getting lost.

- Rental Cars: If renting a car, ensure it's from a reputable agency and always park in well-lit, secure areas.

Avoid Risky Areas and Situations

- Night Safety: Avoid walking alone at night in poorly lit or deserted areas.
- Stay in Busy Areas: Stick to well-populated and popular tourist areas, especially after dark.
- Group Travel: Whenever possible, travel in groups for added safety.

Emergency Information

Local Emergency Numbers

- Emergency Services: Dial 911 for police, fire, or medical emergencies.
- Non-Emergency Police: +1 775-334-2677 (Reno Police Department)

Medical Facilities

- Renown Regional Medical Center: 1155 Mill St, Reno, NV 89502 | +1 775-982-4100
- Saint Mary's Regional Medical Center: 235 W 6th St, Reno, NV 89503 | +1 775-770-3000

Embassy Contacts

For international travelers, knowing the location and contact details of your country's embassy or consulate is crucial in case of emergencies.

- U.S. Embassy: For American citizens, all U.S. consular services are handled through the main embassy in

Washington, D.C., or through the nearest consulate in San Francisco.

- Canadian Consulate General: San Francisco | +1 844-880-6519
- British Consulate General: San Francisco | +1 415-617-1300
- Australian Consulate-General: San Francisco | +1 310-229-2300

Specific Safety Concerns in Reno

Natural Hazards

- Weather Conditions: Reno experiences extreme weather conditions, from hot summers to cold, snowy winters. Dress appropriately and stay hydrated in the heat.
- Wildlife: If exploring outdoor areas, be aware of wildlife and follow local guidelines to avoid encounters.
- Earthquakes: Reno is in an earthquake-prone region. Familiarize yourself with earthquake safety tips and know what to do during a quake.

Local Laws and Customs

- Gambling Regulations: Reno is known for its casinos. Ensure you understand the legal age and regulations for gambling.
- Alcohol Consumption: The legal drinking age is 21. Drink responsibly and be aware of the consequences of public intoxication.
- Smoking Policies: Smoking is prohibited in many public places. Look for designated smoking areas and follow local laws.

Health Risks

- Altitude Sickness: Reno is located at a higher altitude. If you're not accustomed to high altitudes, take it easy for the first few days to avoid altitude sickness.
- Sun Protection: The high elevation means stronger UV rays. Wear sunscreen, hats, and sunglasses to protect against sunburn.
- Vaccinations: No special vaccinations are required for Reno, but ensure your routine vaccinations are up to date.

Common Scams and Tourist Traps

- Fake Tickets: Only buy tickets for events and attractions from official vendors or authorized resellers to avoid counterfeit tickets.
- Street Scams: Be cautious of strangers offering unsolicited help or trying to distract you while an accomplice attempts to steal from you.
- Overcharging: Always check the menu for prices and confirm costs before ordering in restaurants and bars to avoid unexpected charges.

Practical Tips for Navigating Reno Safely

Dress Codes and Entry Fees

- Nightlife Venues: Many nightclubs and casinos have dress codes. Check in advance and dress accordingly to ensure entry.
- Event Entry: Some events and venues may have entry fees. Verify these details before heading out to avoid surprises.

Peak Hours

- Busy Times: Popular attractions, restaurants, and nightlife spots can get crowded during peak hours. Plan your visits during off-peak times for a more relaxed experience.

Parking Tips

- Secure Parking: Use secure parking lots or garages, especially at night. Avoid leaving valuables in your car.
- Street Parking: If parking on the street, always check for signs indicating parking regulations to avoid fines.

By following these safety and security tips, travelers can enjoy a worry-free experience while exploring the vibrant city of Reno. With the right precautions and awareness, you can fully immerse yourself in all that Reno has to offer, from its bustling nightlife to its serene natural landscapes.

Travel Insurance

When planning your trip to Reno, securing travel insurance is a crucial step to ensure a worry-free journey. Travel insurance provides a safety net for unexpected expenses and emergencies, allowing you to enjoy your vacation with peace of mind. This guide highlights the benefits of travel insurance, the different types of policies available, and tips for selecting the right coverage for your needs.

Benefits of Travel Insurance

Medical Emergencies

- Emergency Medical Care: Travel insurance covers medical expenses in case of sudden illness or injury, which can be significantly high without coverage.

- Hospitalization and Treatment: Policies typically include coverage for hospital stays, surgeries, and treatments.
- Medical Evacuation: In severe cases, insurance can cover the cost of medical evacuation to the nearest appropriate facility or back to your home country.

Trip Cancellations or Interruptions

- Cancellation Coverage: Reimbursement for prepaid, non-refundable expenses if you need to cancel your trip due to covered reasons such as illness, natural disasters, or family emergencies.
- Interruption Coverage: Covers the cost of returning home early if your trip is cut short due to an emergency.
- Missed Connections: Compensation for missed connections that lead to additional travel expenses.

Lost or Stolen Belongings

- Baggage Loss or Delay: Coverage for lost, stolen, or damaged baggage and personal items.
- Personal Belongings: Compensation for essential items if your baggage is delayed for an extended period.

Other Unforeseen Circumstances

- Travel Delays: Reimbursement for additional expenses incurred due to travel delays, such as accommodation and meals.
- Accidental Death and Dismemberment: Benefits for serious injuries or death resulting from an accident during your trip.
- Rental Car Coverage: Optional coverage for damages or theft of rental cars.

Types of Travel Insurance Policies

Single Trip Insurance

- Coverage for One Trip: Ideal for travelers planning a single trip. Covers the specific dates and destinations of that trip.
- Comprehensive Options: Includes medical, cancellation, and baggage coverage for the duration of the trip.

Multi-Trip Insurance

- Annual Coverage: Suitable for frequent travelers. Provides coverage for multiple trips within a year.
- Convenience: Eliminates the need to purchase separate policies for each trip.

Comprehensive Plans

- All-Inclusive Coverage: Offers the most extensive protection, including medical emergencies, trip cancellations, baggage, and more.
- Customizable Options: Allows you to add specific coverages based on your needs.

Optional Add-Ons and Upgrades

- Adventure Sports Coverage: Extra coverage for activities like skiing, snowboarding, and other adventure sports.
- Cancel for Any Reason: Offers more flexibility by allowing you to cancel your trip for reasons not covered under standard policies.
- Business Travel Coverage: Additional benefits for business travelers, including coverage for work equipment and trip interruptions due to work-related issues.

Tips for Selecting a Reputable Travel Insurance Provider

Research and Compare

- Reputable Providers: Choose an insurance provider with a strong reputation and positive customer reviews.
- Policy Comparison: Compare policies from multiple providers to find the best coverage and price.

Understand the Terms and Conditions

- Read the Fine Print: Carefully read the policy details to understand what is covered and any exclusions or limitations.
- Claim Process: Familiarize yourself with the process for filing claims and any required documentation.

Coverage Limits and Exclusions

- Maximum Coverage Amounts: Check the maximum payout limits for different types of coverage, such as medical expenses and trip cancellations.
- Exclusions: Be aware of any activities or situations that are not covered by the policy.

Customer Support

- 24/7 Assistance: Choose a provider that offers round-the-clock customer support for emergencies and claims.
- Accessibility: Ensure the provider has accessible contact options, such as phone, email, and online chat.

The Value of Travel Insurance

Travel insurance is a vital component of any trip, offering protection against unexpected events that can disrupt your plans and incur significant costs. Here's why travel insurance is essential:

- Peace of Mind: Knowing that you're covered in case of emergencies allows you to enjoy your trip without constant worry.
- Financial Protection: Coverage for medical emergencies, trip cancellations, and lost belongings can save you from substantial financial losses.
- Assistance Services: Many policies include assistance services that can help you navigate emergencies, such as finding a local doctor or arranging medical transport.

Investing in travel insurance is a smart and essential step in your trip planning process. It ensures that you are prepared for any unexpected events that may arise, allowing you to relax and enjoy your time in Reno. By understanding the different types of policies, carefully selecting a reputable provider, and comprehending the terms and conditions, you can secure the right travel insurance coverage tailored to your needs. Whether you're exploring Reno's vibrant nightlife, hiking its scenic trails, or enjoying its cultural attractions, travel insurance provides the security and peace of mind you need for a memorable and worry-free adventure.

Sustainable Travel Practices

Traveling responsibly and minimizing your environmental impact is increasingly important as tourism grows. Reno offers many opportunities to practice sustainable travel, ensuring that you leave a positive impact on the environment and the local community. Here are some tips and insights to help you travel sustainably in Reno.

Reducing Waste

Use Reusable Water Bottles and Shopping Bags

- Reusable Water Bottles: Bring a reusable water bottle to reduce plastic waste. Many hotels, restaurants, and attractions in Reno have water refill stations.
- Reusable Shopping Bags: Carry reusable bags for shopping to avoid single-use plastics. Many local stores and markets support this eco-friendly practice.

Minimize Single-Use Plastics

- Avoid Plastic Straws: Use reusable or biodegradable straws.
- Pack Reusable Utensils: Bring your own utensils for picnics or take-out meals.

Conserving Energy and Water

In Accommodations

- Energy Conservation: Turn off lights, TV, and air conditioning when not in use. Choose accommodations with energy-saving initiatives, such as LED lighting and smart thermostats.
- Water Conservation: Take shorter showers and reuse towels to conserve water. Some hotels participate in linen reuse programs—be sure to opt-in if available.

Choosing Eco-Friendly Accommodations

- Green Certifications: Look for accommodations with eco-certifications, such as LEED or Green Key.

- Sustainable Practices: Choose hotels that use renewable energy, have recycling programs, and source local, organic food.

Supporting Local Businesses and Artisans

Shopping Local

- Local Markets: Visit local farmers' markets and artisan shops to support Reno's economy and reduce the carbon footprint associated with transporting goods.
- Handmade Crafts: Purchase souvenirs and gifts made by local artisans, which often reflect the region's culture and heritage.

Dining Local

- Farm-to-Table Restaurants: Choose restaurants that source ingredients locally and offer seasonal menus.
- Local Cuisine: Enjoy traditional dishes and support local chefs and food producers.

Choosing Eco-Friendly Transportation

Public Transportation

- Bus Services: Use Reno's public bus system, RTC, which offers extensive routes throughout the city.
- Bike Sharing: Take advantage of bike-sharing programs for a healthy and eco-friendly way to explore.

Carpooling and Ridesharing

- Ridesharing Apps: Use ridesharing services like Uber or Lyft, and choose shared rides when possible to reduce the number of vehicles on the road.

- Carpooling: If renting a car, consider carpooling with other travelers to minimize emissions.

Respecting Wildlife and Natural Habitats

Responsible Wildlife Viewing

- Maintain Distance: Keep a safe distance from wildlife to avoid disturbing them.
- No Feeding: Do not feed animals, as this can harm their health and alter their natural behaviors.

Leave No Trace

- Stay on Trails: Stick to designated trails to prevent damage to vegetation and wildlife habitats.
- Pack Out Trash: Carry out all trash and leave natural areas as you found them.

Sustainable Tourism Initiatives in Reno

Eco-Certified Tour Operators

- Certified Tours: Choose tour operators that are certified by eco-friendly organizations, ensuring they follow sustainable practices.
- Small Group Tours: Opt for small group tours to minimize environmental impact and enhance the quality of your experience.

Volunteering and Community Projects

- Conservation Projects: Participate in community-based conservation projects, such as tree planting or habitat restoration.

- Local Charities: Volunteer with local charities and organizations working to preserve Reno's environment and support its communities.

Practical Tips for Sustainable Travel

Plan Ahead

- Research: Investigate the sustainability practices of hotels, restaurants, and tour operators before booking.
- Pack Light: Travel with minimal luggage to reduce fuel consumption during your journey.

Be Mindful of Your Carbon Footprint

- Carbon Offsetting: Consider offsetting the carbon emissions from your travel by investing in environmental projects.
- Sustainable Flights: Choose direct flights when possible to reduce carbon emissions from take-offs and landings.

Educate and Advocate

- Learn and Share: Educate yourself about the environmental issues facing Reno and share your knowledge with fellow travelers.
- Support Policies: Advocate for sustainable tourism policies and support businesses that prioritize sustainability.

Engaging with Local Initiatives

Participate in Green Events

- Eco-Friendly Events: Attend local events that promote sustainability, such as eco-fairs and clean-up drives.

- Workshops and Talks: Join workshops and talks to learn more about Reno's environmental efforts and how you can contribute.

Connect with Nature

- Nature Reserves: Visit nature reserves and parks that focus on conservation and education.
- Eco-Tours: Take part in eco-tours that emphasize environmental awareness and conservation efforts.

By adopting sustainable travel practices, you can help protect Reno's environment and support its local communities. Reducing waste, conserving energy and water, supporting local businesses, and choosing eco-friendly transportation options are just a few ways to make a positive impact. Additionally, respecting wildlife, participating in sustainable tourism initiatives, and engaging with local conservation efforts can enhance your travel experience and contribute to the preservation of this beautiful destination. Embrace these practices to ensure that future generations can also enjoy the natural and cultural wonders of Reno.

CONCLUSION

Reflecting On Your Reno Adventure

As your journey through Reno comes to an end, it's time to reflect on the many facets of this vibrant city that have made your adventure truly unforgettable. Reno, known as "The Biggest Little City in the World," offers a unique blend of outdoor activities, cultural experiences, culinary delights, and lively entertainment. Here's a look back at some of the highlights that likely made your visit special.

The Natural Beauty and Outdoor Adventures

Reno's location at the base of the Sierra Nevada mountains provides a stunning natural backdrop and endless opportunities for outdoor enthusiasts. Whether you hiked the scenic trails at Mount Rose, skied down the slopes of the nearby Lake Tahoe resorts, or enjoyed a leisurely stroll along the Truckee Riverwalk, the city's natural beauty and adventure offerings are unparalleled. The crisp mountain air and panoramic views undoubtedly rejuvenated your spirit and left you with memories of breathtaking landscapes.

Cultural and Historical Insights

Reno's rich history and vibrant cultural scene have surely enriched your visit. From exploring the exhibits at the Nevada Museum of Art and the National Automobile Museum to wandering through the historic streets of Midtown and experiencing the architectural grandeur of the University of Nevada, Reno, the city's heritage is deeply woven into its fabric. The stories of the early settlers, the rise of the gaming industry, and the artistic renaissance in the arts district have provided a deeper understanding of Reno's unique character.

Culinary Journey

Your taste buds were likely delighted by the diverse culinary landscape of Reno. The farm-to-table restaurants, vibrant food markets, and innovative eateries showcase the city's commitment to fresh, local ingredients and creative cuisine. Whether savoring Basque-inspired dishes, indulging in gourmet food trucks, or enjoying a cozy café breakfast, Reno's food scene offers something for every palate. The city's burgeoning brewery and winery scene added another layer of flavor to your visit, with local brews and wines providing a true taste of Nevada.

Entertainment and Nightlife

Reno's entertainment and nightlife are as dynamic as they come. The city's renowned casinos, such as the Grand Sierra Resort and Casino and the Eldorado Resort Casino, provided thrilling gaming experiences and world-class shows. The vibrant nightlife scene, with its eclectic mix of bars, clubs, and live music venues, ensured your evenings were filled with excitement and discovery. The Riverwalk District, in particular, stands out for its lively atmosphere, offering a perfect blend of entertainment, dining, and scenic views.

Community and Local Interaction

One of the most rewarding aspects of your Reno adventure was likely the interaction with the local community. Renown for their friendliness and hospitality, the people of Reno made you feel welcome and at home. Whether chatting with local artisans at markets, learning about sustainable practices from eco-tour operators, or engaging in conversations with fellow travelers and residents, these connections added a personal touch to your experience.

Unique Experiences

Reno is a city of hidden gems and off-the-beaten-path attractions. Discovering lesser-known spots like the historic Bruka Theatre, exploring the vibrant street art in the Riverwalk District, or finding peace in the serenity of the Wilbur D. May Arboretum and Botanical Garden are experiences that truly set Reno apart. These unique adventures enriched your visit, offering glimpses into the city's eclectic charm and diverse offerings.

Sustainability and Responsible Travel

Throughout your journey, the emphasis on sustainable travel practices in Reno likely stood out. From choosing eco-friendly accommodations and transportation options to supporting local businesses and artisans, your efforts contributed to the preservation and growth of the city's environment and economy. Participating in conservation projects or simply making conscious choices helped you leave a positive impact on Reno, ensuring that future visitors can also enjoy its beauty and culture.

Final Thoughts

As you reflect on your Reno adventure, it's clear that this city offers a multifaceted experience that caters to a wide range of interests and preferences. The blend of natural beauty, cultural richness, culinary diversity, and vibrant entertainment creates a destination that is both dynamic and welcoming. Whether you came for the outdoor adventures, the historical insights, the nightlife, or simply to relax and unwind, Reno has likely exceeded your expectations and left you with a treasure trove of memories.

In conclusion, Reno is more than just a gateway to the Sierra Nevada; it's a destination in its own right, brimming with opportunities for exploration and discovery. As you return home, the echoes of your Reno adventure will resonate, reminding you of the many moments of joy, discovery, and connection that defined your visit. Until next time, the Biggest Little City in the World awaits your return for another unforgettable journey.

Made in the USA
Coppell, TX
06 August 2024

35680992R00140